To Barbara
and Mary!
Sempre avanti.

9/20/10

The Attack on the White Male

- and The Weakening of America -

STEPHEN L. DEFELICE, M.D.

authorHOUSE®

AuthorHouse™
1663 Liberty Drive
Bloomington, IN 47403
www.authorhouse.com
Phone: 1-800-839-8640

First published by AuthorHouse   6/23/2010

ISBN: 978-1-4520-1098-4 (e)
ISBN: 978-1-4520-1096-0 (sc)
ISBN: 978-1-4520-1097-7 (hc)

Library of Congress Control Number: 2010905969

Printed in the United States of America
Bloomington, Indiana

This book is printed on acid-free paper.

To my beautiful wife Patrice
If she were still by my side, she would warn, "My husband of fifty years,
I forbid you to have this book published. You have fought many big
battles in your life and, at your age, you don't need another one."

But now that she is gone, I will first thank her for her loving concern
and then ask for her forgiveness.

Contents

Why This Book

"Know thyself"

Socrates

O ur grandson, Maximilian, came to live with my wife and me when he was an early teenager. By the time you read this book he will probably be out on his own – somewhere in this new and increasingly virtual world. My wife, Mrs. DeFelice (notice- no first name which gives you a hint where I'm coming from), and I were suddenly exposed to a whole new aggressive world where many forces are hitting all of our brains.

I met many new world folks but the group that grabbed my attention the most was late teen age and early 20's men. I met them in my home, the coffee shop where I do some of my writing and in the homes of others - both where I live and in other cities. I didn't attend any parties where the "grinding" type of sex simulation dance is now commonplace and accepted by schools and parents. The greatest percentage came from middle to upper class families. Most were Caucasian and only a small number were Asiatic, Black or Hispanic. I did have conversations with women in this age group but not as many so I don't have nearly as good a handle of what's going on with them as I do with the young men. But, let me quickly add, I did make some observations particularly when it relates to young women's interactions with men which is, as you well know, a major force influencing you guys.

So this book is mainly about the young white males but also included are some thoughts and observations on other male and female categories. The primary reason why I wrote the book has to do with how modern times are powerfully and rapidly changing the traditional concept of what a man should be. Most of you are not even aware what and how it's happening and what to do about it. You may or may not like what's happening and that's your choice. But you should at least be aware of the forces that are changing you. As far as I am concerned I'm firmly convinced that it's not the best of news not only for you personally but for our country. In my opinion, the conditions contributing to your weakness have led to the weakening of our country. The men today are not as tough as when I was young the main reason being that much of normal masculine behavior is now prohibited.

You may be wondering why I chose this male age group. It is simply based on my personal observation that men in this group can absorb advice, think about it and, if they agree, make firm decisions to put into action that which favorably impacts their lives and country. Those who are younger are not capable of doing this. Those who are older are, and this did surprise me, already fixed in their ways and lose a lot of their flexibility which is necessary to make important changes in their behavior. Of course, there are always exceptions to the rules.

Some of you may be wondering if there was a specific event that got my energy levels high enough to put my pen to this book. There certainly was, and it has to do with baby dolls.

One night as my wife and I were having our usual pre-dinner cocktail, our grandson came walking through the door with a female baby doll dangling from his hand. We, observing this, exchanged glances silently communicating and wondering what this was all about hoping for the best and expecting the worst.

Well, here's what happened. The school wanted to teach teenagers an important sex lesson regarding the price one pays for having babies. The students were told to carry the baby dolls with them around the clock for a week hoping that this would discourage unprotected sexual intercourse.

Now this didn't sit well with me for it was one clear example of how our educational system is feminizing young males. From where I come from, a doll is a girly thing so I called the principal, a nice guy who, in turn, referred me to the woman who handles this sex program. She was very professional and told me that this was a mandatory policy of a number of schools and the boys had no choice.

What really hit me like a thunderbolt was when I asked her how many parents objected to the program. There was none.

This single event symbolized the larger anti-male movement in our country and led me to write this book.

WARNING: After reading this book many will undoubtedly call me a bigot, misogynist (men that hate women or even women that hate women), irreligious, homophobe, right wing racist and so on and so forth all of which is not at all true, particularly the misogynist label. In our age it is difficult to be intellectually honest without being attacked particularly when supporting white males.

DMS: The Demasculinization Syndrome

"I don't sit down and pee"

Larry David

After reading this chapter a very high percentage of the readers with all different kinds of outlooks of life will come together. Not only will they strongly and even passionately dislike what I have to say but some will also dislike me personally. As I said before, what is interesting is that some will think I'm one or more of the following: an atheist, a racist, an anti-feminist and misogynist (women hater) cynic, a very right conservative, a macho man, a homophobe and decadent doctor - among others. It will surprise them that I do not fall into any of those categories, except one in the "among others" category, which is a private matter and privacy, guys, is a precious thing.

Now why will folks have these opinions and feelings? It's because I am trying to tell the truth and never forget very few people can handle the truth particularly when it comes close to their emotional home. When people already have their fixed and particularly really passionate ideas, they are comfortable living with them, and it takes a hell of a lot of ammunition to change even one. Remember, Aristotle defined man as a rational creature. DeFelice defines a man as a creature who rationalizes. In our country, the influence peddlers or marketeers such as the media, government, educational institutions and businesses are playing a huge role not only pushing their values on all of us but also figuring out how they should counterattack if someone challenges their messages. We are in an outright cultural war where the anti-you forces are everywhere you look.

For example, if I say that women should not be in submarines, the immediate reaction would be that I'm an anti-feminist or misogynist. If I also say that the affirmative action movement has gone way too far, I will immediately be labeled as a racist and a misogynist combined. If I say that white males are being discriminated against, as I say in this book, all hell would break through and the counter attacks launched.

Everyone, you and everybody else, has and is being big time brainwashed. Many will react to this statement as an exaggeration. Baloney! And, let me keep emphasizing, that you guys are the ones taking the biggest hit for the simple reason you are clearly losing in the competition.

Jesus once said, "The truth shall make you free." And that's what you are being deprived of and that's what you're going to read about in this book. Amen!

Before we go on let me tell you one story from when I was a young man about how I learned how difficult it is to change someone's mind by the use of reason. When I was a student at Central High School in Philadelphia, a great all boys school in those days, I took courses in rhetoric, which I really loved. Basically, rhetoric is the art, by debating, of proving someone wrong by the use of reason even though your opponent may be right! In my debates with a lot of smart, gutsy guys, I learned a lot about the way people think. I would highly recommend that those of you who are potential leaders take a course in rhetoric for it will immensely help you in the battle of both selling your ideas and disproving those of others.

During the first lecture my intellectually challenging teacher told me an eye-opening story that had a major and lasting impact on me regarding the limited power of the use of reason. It's one of those moments that ordinarily you wouldn't be impressed with but for some particular reason it really woke me up. I'm sure some of you know what I'm talking about. Regarding such moments, a Catholic Jesuit priest, who was highly trained in the use of rhetoric and his close friend, a romantic Hindu poet from India, had a wonderful dinner one night along with a few drinks. The Hindu was a bit of a rebel for his religious sect prohibits the intake of booze. As they sat down for dinner the romantic Hindu smiled and said to his Jesuit companion, "My friend, there are exceptions to every rule" and they then ordered a bottle of wine. They talked about lots of things including the great question of what is the meaning of life.

After dinner they ordered a cognac and afterwards split the bill and then left the restaurant. It was a beautiful night without a cloud in the sky. There was a brilliant full moon, which poets love to describe in poems regarding young lovers with hormones flowing. Jimmy Durante, an actor comedian way back before you were born repeatedly said in his act, "How sweet it is!"

(I sometimes wonder why there are few, if any, poems written about elderly lovers, and they are around, under the same romantic moon. Why not ask your mom and dad)?

Gazing at the sky the Jesuit said to his friend, "My God, isn't the moon beautiful tonight?" His good friend then looked him straight in the eyes and surprisingly answered, "What moon?" The first instinct of the Jesuit was that he was joking around, but he wasn't. His second instinct was that, by using his rhetorical skills, it would be easy to prove to his friend that the moon was there filling the night with romantic light, clearly visible above them. He first pointed his finger toward the moon and said, "That moon. You must see it, my friend." The Hindu replied, "I'm sorry my friend but I don't see it." When the Jesuit was about to try to prove his point, he, which really surprised him, found himself lost for words and didn't know what to say. He couldn't, with words, prove the obvious. I don't remember how the story between the two ended but I remember very well the lesson I learned. It's very, very tough to convince the vast majority of people of the obvious if they don't want to believe it. So don't get frustrated and accept what it is. If you try and fail, just smile and change the subject.

What I'm going to talk about now are some examples of how modern times are screwing up people in general but more specifically about how you are losing in the competitive battle for power. *And what you should be very aware of is that almost all of you don't even know how much of a beating you're taking because no one is telling you!*

Look, I'm not going to bore you with a lengthy analysis of what's going on and will keep it very brief so get out of cyberspace for awhile, and let's talk about some powerful and growing large movements that are going against you. So pay close attention, and let's move forward.

Never since the Big Bang and Higg's boson (the particle that gave mass to the universe including you) happened about 14 billion years ago and the earth about 4.5 billion (that's when some say that God created the Universe, including earth, in six days and took a break on the seventh), has there been a more dramatic change on human behavior and destiny as is going on today. Not only is technology taking control of our lives but it now has the capacity to exterminate all planet life in a nuclear instant or a little bit more slowly by biological warfare. We don't need giant dinosaur-killing meteors anymore to do the job.

We all know that there are power seeking leaders out there involved in developing and controlling weapons of mass destruction far more devastating than current ones. There's a saying or maybe a poem where it states, "Eat, drink and be merry, for tomorrow we die." This may be farfetched and maybe sometimes not.

But there's something at this point in time, would you believe in the United States, that's really seems to be coming our way. It is the control of human behavior itself from the mental to the physical. To repeat over and over again in order to get the message into your brains, there are the "marketeer groups" or mind-controllers that are all over the place selling their idea and products to you and everyone else through our huge overwhelming indoctrination system – and, take my word, it is overwhelming - and you must be aware of what it's doing to your head. Controlling your thoughts, judgments and style of living makes it extremely difficult to think on your own and, like a thief in the night, is gradually making you lose your freedom. Whether you know it or not, you are much less free now than when I was a young man, and, it's your call, whether you want to fight the monster. And in order to do this it requires leaders to lead the battle charge. More about this later.

There is another part of what's going on that you must watch out for. It is very difficult these days for you to know the truth from what you hear, see and read. The more media input the more persuasive untruths facts flow to your brains. Mark Twain said, "If you don't read newspapers, you are not informed. If you do, you are misinformed." Yes, you can know that Snoop Dog has a great new video but what about larger things that really impact our country such as what's going on with the Supreme Court or in Afghanistan or in the economy? Take my word for it, the truth simply ain't there or is distorted by those folks who have an agenda and want something for themselves. For example, smearing a person's reputation is a tactic used. In my interviews with high school students in several schools I was told by both the guys and gals that nasty and oftentimes vicious rumors are commonly spread usually, by the way, by the female students, to hurt someone. It's done all the time in politics and by the real experts, the media, oftentimes in subtle ways that you can't detect and fool you.

Now let's take a brief, general look at some aspects of this competitive race and why you are now on the losing side.

Politics and Politicians

Let me clearly state that it's easy, no, very easy, to be cynical about our politicians. Even the term "politician" carries with it some shady overtones like you can't trust the guy or he'll do double-dealing to advance his self-interest. I met a guy at a birthday party by a poolside one sunny afternoon who told me how he spent a frustrating year in Congress trying to get a new law passed or enacted. Shortly after he took a big sip of the heavily spiked punch, he said, "Don't go away. Wait a minute." He went into his house and then came out with a lighted flashlight. I couldn't figure out what he was looking for because the sun was brilliant, and we could see everything without the need of additional light. After I told him that, he smiled and said he often felt like the ancient Cynic Greek philosopher, Diogenes, while he was in Washington political circles. Diogenes famously walked around with a lighted lamp during the day and when asked by the curious crowd what he was up to, he answered, "I'm searching for an honest man!"

Now let me tell you the truth about politicians for they have had and are currently dramatically increasing their immense influence on everyone's life and in a particularly negative way on yours. I am not cynical about them for the nature of their jobs makes them do what they do. Let's just say, I'm disappointed.

Though there are exceptions and I know a few - try not go into ecstasy and get too excited over a political figure and his or her promises for they rarely can or are willing to deliver on their promises. The political system just simply won't permit it for they are not kings with absolute power. Also, the vast majority are not visionaries with firm beliefs and principles like our Founding Fathers but ambitious people who seek the thrill of power along with job security. The major objectives of a politician are to get elected and stay elected. Certain politicians have concluded that the way to do that is to get enough votes by catering to target groups by passing laws and using indirect ways to establish quota systems. Among these groups are women, blacks and other minority groups.

You guys are on the very bottom of the list of influentials.

Over the years, since I have had lots of experience in Washington, many have asked me how a politician can make promises while running for election and then, when elected, turn around and do the opposite or even forget about it. Most normal folks just couldn't behave this way.

For years I thought about it but didn't have an answer until I read one of Italy's greatest novels, *Il Gattopardo* or *The Leopard*. The main character was a rich Sicilian aristocrat who was asked to run for an important government office. He refused. When asked the reason why he replied, "I lack the quality of self-deception." Now, from time to time, we all deceive ourselves in life trying to justify our actions that deep down we are uncomfortable with. The politicians take this art to a much higher level.

And now a personal confession: I have had and still have politicians who are my friends. As my father told me, "It takes all kinds to make a world."

Civil Rights, Affirmative Action, Feminists, Women's Liberation, Diversity and Political Correctness

Cyberspace and other sources contain more information on these subjects than your and my mind can both absorb and analyze. So let me very briefly get to the heart of the matter of the message for each category. If you are one of those who would prefer to smoke a joint and/or sniff a line and gaze at your belly button rather than learning about what's going on, then that's your call. You can take a horse to water but you can't make him drink.

Civil Rights-Affirmative Action: What I'm talking about here are the laws passed by Congress that minority groups, primarily the black community, should be given special "rights" not only because they were treated as second class citizens in the past but also to catch up to you because you have dominated American culture in every aspect since the Pilgrims arrived on New England shores when Pocahontas and John Smith met and went bananas over each other. This movement is primarily aimed at you and not your lady counterparts because, at that time, most of the jobs and students at universities were held by white males. The result of the Civil Rights Movement has been and continues to be implemented and highly effective. Enrollment in universities and job employment in corporations of blacks has gone beyond the wildest dreams of the distinguished crusader, Martin Luther King, and we now have President Obama elected by enthusiastic white Americans. On the other hand, I wish this historic good man, Dr. King, were still around to hear what he has to say about what's been going on with his disciples and whether he would be happy about them.

Now get this into your head: The result of this movement made legitimate the concept of QUOTAS or reverse discrimination. Now follow me on this issue: Quotas deal with fixed percentages. A college and a business must enroll or hire a certain percentage of blacks or lose federal funding.

You can argue until you're blue in the face whether affirmative action has benefited our country. What is clear, however, is that you guys have been beaten up in all kinds of ways including lost opportunities to be admitted to universities and to be hired at a job. This policy has worked against you because your academic performance and labor skills have now taken a secondary role to the color of one's skin and, as we shall see, the sex gender.

Not too long ago, the Supreme Court ruled against the quota system in certain cases. But it has become so ingrained in our culture that it still goes on and now appears to be, Supreme Court or not, almost irreversible.

Feminist-Women's Liberation: This movement has done not only what the original affirmative action movement has done for blacks but much, much more. It is changing the nature of man-woman relationships including massive disintegration of family life and "where she stops nobody knows". In particular, by changing what mothers used to be, the strong foundation and managers of family life, it has had a huge destructive impact on all children let alone on husbands and wives. Divorce is now a snap when compared to the past when it was real difficult to get one except if you were a Hollywood movie star. Many of you who are products of divorced parents know what I'm talking about.

The powerful women's liberation movement has been a spectacular success when you judge it by certain objective standards. It is estimated that within a few years there will be one hundred fifty women students to one hundred males in our higher learning institutions. Corporations, the vast majority controlled by men, have raced to hire more female employees in high-level positions sometimes even exceeding the number of men. Women now purchase fifty per cent of all cars by themselves and are involved in selecting the cars of their husbands about fifty per cent of the time. Women spend a lot more bucks than men so corporations market heavily to them. The majority of single and divorced women leans left and votes for Democrats. The majority of white males leans right and votes Republican. Women read much more than men and, for this reason, are more susceptible to the influence of the mind controlling marketeers.

The inescapable conclusion is that the women's liberation movement is giving you a competitive beating. And would you believe it, as with our black countrymen, despite the tremendous advances of both groups, the laws and social pressures still exist to further their cause and diminish yours. And, puzzling as it may seem, there are no energetic, effective male leaders or groups to say, "It's enough" and get rid of these special privileges feeding their self-interest. The marketeers, government, corporations, universities and women's groups, media among others, continue to be the competitive winners and press forward with their anti-you causes.

But, as with anything in life you always pay the price when you believe and get something that you feel happy about. Let me tell you a story what happened to me when I was, as a doctor, drafted during the Vietnam War. I arrived at Fort Sam Houston in Texas when the desert temperature was sky high. While I was in line to sign in, I met the guy behind me who was a psychiatrist at the famous medical institution, Johns Hopkins. We got to talk about various things such as the probability we would be killed in the Vietnam jungle because we, being mechanical morons, could not master the compass and might walk in the wrong direction right into the Viet Cong camp. Later on we found out that this indeed happened to one of the doctors we trained with. We never found out what happened to him. He was a nice guy who hated his compass.

After I signed in I was told I had an option either to stay on the military base or get a room somewhere in a local motel. Well, I decided to get my own pad and enjoy as much as I could of what might be my last moments on planet earth. I rented a car and found a motel about ten miles from the camp. I checked in, walked to my room and had just put the key in the door slot when I heard someone behind me doing the same thing at the room across from mine. I turned around, and, would you believe, it was the doctor whom I met when I was signing up. We both laughed and became close friends during our Fort Sam Houston days. We decided to have some good times together but the only available way to have it in those days was at dinner time with good food and spirits - the latter, in case you don't know it, means booze.

We were lucky for we managed to find a good French restaurant, and we ate there frequently. It happened one night when we went overboard and drank way over our limits. We ordered two bottles of my then favorite French white burgundy, Corton Charlemagne. And we had one of those wonderful beautiful moments in life talking about everything from the meaning of life, how to master the use of a compass and to what the hell were we doing in Vietnam.

Well the next morning we got up early to go to the fort to do the marching exercises under the blazing sun and desert heat. Both of us had huge hangovers, and I mean huge! After we talked and even laughed about our hangovers, he philosophically said, "Steve, we always have to pay the price in life. Life is that way. We had a good time but now we must pay the price". The ancient Greeks agreed. They believed that the best way to punish a man is for the gods to grant him what he wishes. And take my word for it; there's a lot of truth to it.

Some are of the opinion, though many will not agree, that women, by winning in the competition, have paid a heavier price than men and the country has also suffered because of this. I'll talk more about this later on.

There are "rights" movements all over the place such as rights to health care and rights to an education. The courts have generally gone along with those demanding more rights. Don't forget, as I'll discuss later on, no one has any rights except those that you have at a point in time. They come and go like the four seasons. And you are in competition to win the rights battle. Remember this important principle: *When you give a right to someone, you take a right away from someone else!*

Diversity: This is the hottest current movement that is working against you, more than most of you probably imagine. Remember what I just said; if you give a right to someone, you take it away from another. Well, that is what diversity does, and you are the major victim of it. Diversity generally means that lots of different types of chosen groups are, as a policy, represented in schools or corporations and other organizations while others are excluded. For example, universities and corporations should have Asians, Arabs, Hispanics, American Indians, blacks, women, gays (but not polygamists) and others types from the brightest to the not so smart. It is another powerful quota system in disguise that is not your friend - not at all.

It's a buzzword that's getting almost everyone "feeling good" about it. Recently, a white male high school student, a solid young lad, asked my advice on how to increase his odds in getting accepted to a college where he was dying, and I mean dying, to be accepted. I asked him why he was so hot on this school. His eyes lighted up, and he answered, "Diversity". It's one of the most diversified in the United States." When I asked him why he was so turned on by the diversity thing, he answered, "It makes me feel good. We are all different types of people all together sharing all of our feelings and getting to know each other better."

Many universities now have diversity weekends where all types of underrepresented or minority students gather together in an attempt to encourage them to apply to the university. Rarely, are white male students permitted to attend. I was told about a white male who pretended to be one-fourth Cherokee Indian. He attended a diversity weekend and was readily accepted by the same institution probably because of his Indian heritage because he was a lousy student.

The truth is that the word "diversity" is a neutral one. Its meaning depends on the situation. For example, if you want to become a doctor or engineer, you want to go to a university where there is a diversity of the best students and teachers in order for you to be really good at what you do. You don't want to be with a diverse population of students based on sex, race and skin color who are not the best.

Sure, there are excellent schools with diversity policies. Look, diversity can be a beautiful thing as long as it's not anti-you. Unfortunately, practically all of it is a disguised anti-you quota system.

There's a very interesting recent phenomenon that's going on regarding female university students. In a diversity attempt to enroll female students, some universities believe they overshot the mark where there are now three females to every two males. Now this can lead to some serious problems with women due to biological and other factors which I'll let you figure out. Now guess what? Would you believe that these schools are now making a significant effort to enroll white male students! But don't be fooled. They are doing this not because they love and miss you guys but only to solve a potentially big problem. They are concerned that the too few men will make the social life of the women, let's say, relatively manless and make them become "players", if you know what I mean.

Now here's a specific example of the power of the diversity quota-system movement that scares the hell out of me. And I don't scare easily. It's going on at one of our great military institutions, the U.S. Naval Academy. It now has a race-based, two-tiered admissions policy where about one third of the student cadets who are admitted must be in the minority group category.

According to a professor at the academy some aspects of the policy are as follows: White applicants, in order to be considered for admission, must have A's and B's as marks and score high on certain sections of the SAT. If, however, you're Hispanic, Black, Native- American Indian or Asian, your marks and SAT scores can be considerably lower. And if a minority student's academic performance is way, way down he's still alive. The Navy will pay to send them to the Naval Academy Preparatory School, which is a remedial teaching institution to give the guy a second chance to enter the Academy.

Now here's the scary part for liberals, conservatives and everybody else in our country. The professor said that a very high official at the Academy said, "Diversity is our number one priority." Just step back and think about this difficult to believe policy. Shouldn't the number one priority be to have the best, most competent naval officers as possible to manage personnel and complex weapon systems ranging from nuclear submarines to cruise missiles and, yes, to Navy Seals. China and other countries are now building up their military at a rapid rate, and I don't need to tell you that they're enlisting their best men and women to be number one or at least at the top of the heap. They are out to beat us for that's the way nations are. We are in a worldwide competition against other nations not only to protect ourselves defensively but to have sufficient offensive capability to serve our national interest- which means all of us. I can tell you that our competitor nations know about this and are as happy as a pig in shit that we are dummying down our military by reverse discrimination against white males which is weakening our country. And what is very, very disturbing is the virtual absence of leaders to sound the alarm. Have you ever wondered why?

In addition to dummying down our military might there remains the issue of big-time discrimination policy. But, unlike women and blacks who would stir the waters and try to reverse this policy if it were against them, you guys are like tongueless sheep that don't give a peep. You remain silent on the sidelines losing to your competitors.

Before I go on, let me tell you about a real life story where I was personally involved. I have a friend who is a single mom who is rearing a solid son who was accepted to a number of universities and in the process of selecting his choice.

She invited me to attend a reception at a major university for accepted students who had not yet made their final decisions. The auditorium was huge and filled to capacity with potential students, families and friends.

There was a student body ratio of three females to two males. I made a quick survey of the audience and observed that males were hard to find. I concluded that this class would indeed increase the female to male ratio.

The reception was opened by a female student. The major speaker was a female dean. At the end of her welcoming remarks she referred to two historic figures as examples of persons to look up to and emulate, and they were excellent choices. The first was Martin Luther King and the second was, I can't remember her name, perhaps the first woman doctor who graduated from a medical school in our country.

I was expecting that she would then refer to a white male as a role model such as George Washington or Abraham Lincoln. None was mentioned.

By midday my friend's son was unabashedly approached by four prospective female students asking him for his phone number and email address. In addition, a mother aggressively tried to hook him up with her daughter. Though I should have envied him, I, instead, felt both sorrow and concern for him thinking how difficult it would be to maintain his high scholastic performance if he enrolled there.

Politically correct and not politically correct: Generally speaking, these terms are used in different ways. For example, if someone says or does things that are true but hurt the feelings and sensitivities of others, it is "not politically correct". If, however, one does not do this then "it is politically correct". It is an increasingly powerful tool to control free speech and behavior of practically everyone but, here we go again, against you in particular. An example of political incorrectness hit the national scene a few years ago when the President of Harvard, Lawrence Summers, made a casual remark in private that he believes men were better at theoretical sciences such as mathematics than women which certainly appears to be true. Men are mostly leading the way in computer and technology advances such as the leaders of Microsoft, Google and Yahoo among others. Well, the- you-know –what hit the fan. Women on the Harvard faculty with feminist values, joined by some of their girlymen male colleagues, went bananas demanding, would you believe, that he resign for his disparaging, politically incorrect anti-women remarks. Practically the entire national media covered the story getting anti-Summers quotes from women's groups and others. Where were the men to support him, you ask? A couple, and I mean only a couple, of isolated males supported Summers and the poor guy was left to hang on his own. He tried to explain, and even apologized, which didn't help his image, to various groups explaining that he was just making an intellectual judgment and was not biased against women. To no avail! The Harvard faculty and the media and women support groups continued the pressure until Mr. Summers was forced to resign. Fortunately, the guy's career wasn't finished yet, and he is, at this moment, one of President Obama's chief financial advisers.

Let's now look at another potential scenario. If Mr. Summers would have said that he believed, though there is absolutely no evidence, that he thought women were superior to men at mathematics this also would have also made national headlines but in a positive way even pleasing the women and girlymen at Harvard and the many marketeers who support them. A typical headline would read, "The President of Harvard Believes Women are Superior to Men in Mathematics." He would have been praised by almost every segment of the university community, women's groups and become a "star" in the mass media which, by the way, is controlled, would you believe, by men. And what would we hear from the male community? Zero! It is not in the nature of men to organize lots of big or even small protest groups. For example, there are tons of women television talk shows where they discuss lots of things including themselves and oftentimes beat up on men. I haven't found one male show that is similar. In fact, I haven't found an all male talk show at all. This male characteristic, the reluctance to organize effective groups and communicate through mass media to voice their opinions and have substantial impact against the marketeers, makes you much less competitive with women and other minorities in molding our national values.

Now let's take a look at political correctness in the black community. Before we do so I'd like to tell you a story of my teenager experiences when I was sixteen years old. I got a job in one of the big supermarkets in a rich section in a Philadelphia food supermarket which was very far away from my home. It took me a little less than four hours round trip to work back to home. I'm talking about the mid- 1950's, a long time ago when most things moved slowly and our country was strong.

Some of the customers were big-time snobs and would occasionally bust my chops. A couple of times I wanted to kick them in the rear end and push them out of the store. One day a middle aged woman dressed to the nines with her nose held high in the air asked me in a haughty, condescending tone, "Where are the *tomatt-toes*" and not tomatoes. The former is the British pronunciation which was supposed to elevate her image as a sophisticated woman but she really didn't have it. I told her we didn't have *tomatt-toes* but we only sold tomatoes.

She complained to the manager and, looking back, he did me a big favor. He transferred me to a very small store in a black community in the heart of the city. My boss was a buxom white lady with a great sense of humor, and we got along very well with the customers. By the way, she felt safe and had no fears walking the streets of the neighborhood. What we experienced were folks with a wonderful sense of humor and a total absence of anger. Drug pushers were not around in those days but booze intake was healthy.

For a number of reasons, some of which are justified, the Civil Rights movement fueled anger and resentment in the black community spurred on by their leaders. But, as the great scientist, Isaac Newton discovered in physics, for every action there is an equal reaction. This principle roughly applies to human behavior. Think about this. Anyway, the white community reacted with anger and resentment for understandable reasons for the new laws created abuses in the system one being "playing the race card". Briefly, as I said before, the new laws gave blacks advantages over whites in many areas from getting into college to getting jobs by setting up a quota system or reverse discrimination. The intent was to make up for the very widespread historic discrimination against blacks. Playing the racial card simply means that one uses these laws and public sentiment to their upmost advantage to help their self- interest.

A long time ago, before the sperms and eggs that made you were not yet made, I was invited to appear on The Good Morning America television show. All the guests that would appear were seated in a waiting room waiting to be called. Sitting next to me was a pissed-off white businessman who was approached by someone on the TV staff who asked him a few questions before he went on the air after my interview. The businessman – notice, I didn't write businessperson which would be politically correct- claimed that he couldn't fire an incompetent black worker because of the new laws that Congress had passed. He said something like, "This guy is 'playing the race card' and we must make this clear because that what's happening these days." The TV guy became a little uncomfortable and told him not to use the phrase regarding the racial card but some other language. The guy asked why not because it is what it is. The TV guy answered that it would offend blacks and other people who are sensitive to racial issues; in other words, it's not politically correct and, once more, the truth cannot be told.

This may surprise you but, if I were a black employee, I would probably do the same thing out of my self-interest. If the law is there that gives me a competitive advantage such as the "white card", I wouldn't be too intelligent if I didn't take advantage of it. After all, I need a job to make money for me and to support my family. It's a self-interest legitimate survival issue and only fools would ignore this advantage. It's plain Darwinian evolutionary theory which holds that there is no such thing as being fair be it in the jungle or the civilized human world.

By the way, after Obama was elected president which was a welcomed historical sign that the race issue ain't what it used to be, a couple of big time black politicians, one incompetent and the other corrupt, tried to use the race card to protect their rear ends. They both flopped in their attempt. Thank God for it helps diminish the unnecessary anger and hatred in our country in these difficult times! But it is not nearly enough. The laws remain on the books despite the fact that black Americans have now become an integral part of the American system. We shall see what the future holds.

There are, in spirit, extensions of the politically correct movement; one of the most serious is Congress's attempt to regulate hate crimes and limit your freedom of speech. According to current law, a hate crime involves those actions motivated by the victim's color, religion, race or national origins. Congress is now trying to broaden the language to include homosexuals and transgender people. For example, if, let's say, a Quaker elder from the pulpit, in a very passionate sermon, severely criticizes gay rights to marry. Then one of the parishioners goes out and beats up a gay guy. It will be up to the police and courts to decide whether the elder had hate in his mind as the motive for the criticism which incited the guy to attack. If they agree, the elder could go to jail even though he was not angry at the gays but only at the law. Also, they will have to figure out what's the difference between anger and hate and which one was in the Quaker's mind. Don't laugh. This could and probably will happen if we keep going on our current path.

The Vote

Just a reminder: no matter how well meaning and sincere politicians are, bottom line, it's primarily about getting the vote. And to date getting the vote frequently results in increasing attacks on you.

Religion: Recent Surveys
I will give you my thoughts on religion a little later but there is a new book that deals with your age group. It reports the results of the author's survey, the National Study of Youth and Religion, which you should know and think about. Statistical methods were used to objectively measure what's going on. The author of the book, *Souls in Transition*, Christian Smith, is a sociologist at Notre Dame University, a Catholic institution.

Interestingly enough, I was pleasantly surprised by the results. I thought they would be less favorable to religion. But let me tell you that many out there in our country were disappointed hoping that the results would be less favorable.

Some of the results are as follows:

1. About twenty per cent of young Americans go to church at least once a week, significantly less than five years ago.

2. What really hit me is that most of these young adults said that when they get older and have children they intend to rear their children in the faith of their parents. This means that parents still and will have lots of influence on their children which is very good news.

3. Regarding what's right and wrong, the non-religious group had no objective standards to make these judgments and relied on "feeling". In other words, though they may not realize this, anything goes for feelings differ with different people. What's important for you to know is that the religious group is far more confident in their judgments of what is right and wrong because they have God, an objective standard, to guide them.

4. I want you to pay particular attention to this: the survey reported that the religious group was more happy, did better at school, was much more inclined to help others and be charitable, took fewer drugs, drank and smoked less, was less depressed, less obese and more likely to go to college. Who can argue with this?

Shortly after this book was published, there was a survey conducted by *Parade*. Parade is a mini-magazine that is inserted in many newspapers and is one of the most widely read publications in our country. Now listen to these results: 69% of Americans believe in God, 77% pray and 75% believe it is the responsibility of parents to educate their children about religion. And why do they pray? 72%

for the well being of others, 60% for forgiveness, 27% for personal success and 21% for material things such as money.

Now I don't know about you guys but I think these results should get you thinking about things. Also, it's useful information for you to use when the passionate anti-religion folks irrationally attack religion. Act like a professor and say something like, "Do you know of the book Souls and Tradition and the Parade Survey? " Religion, God or no God, is a crutch in life that fools ignore. Those who deny it have emotional or hormonal problems.

The Constitution Should Be Your Friend

Now don't turn your brain off on this issue for the modern interpretation of it is largely responsible for the anti-you movement.

How many times have you heard someone say, "It's unconstitutional"? And how many times did you know or anyone else know what in god's name the person was talking about? I'll bet that well over ninety per cent of the time no one had the slightest idea and yet the Constitution is the cornerstone of not only of United States law but also spells out the ground rules on how we live together as best we can and remain free and strong as a nation. It is, in my opinion, perhaps the greatest political-philosophic document ever written. The Founding Fathers who wrote it were brilliant students of history and what motivates people to do what they do and try to figure out how to turn into a positive national force. For example, they concluded that greed and envy are the major forces that drive human behavior. So they decided that we must convert these powerful destructive forces feelings into positive ones by following the Constitution which permits certain rights such as freedom of speech, the right to own property and commercial or business freedom. And, judged by history, those very wise and strong men read and understood the book of human behavior beyond all others in history. Have any of your teachers or whatever you read and hear about ever taught or informed you about the principles of the Constitution and why it works? The sad news is that almost everyone that I've spoken to about this could not tell me the reasons why which, in a sense, is an opportunity for you guys.

Don't worry, I 'm not about to write a beginner's lesson on this subject but I do want to touch on how the courts, particularly our Supreme Court, have ignored this document in some of its decisions in such a way which stacks the deck of cards against you in life's competition.

When a Supreme Court justice is sworn in, he or she makes a pledge to honor the principles of the Constitution. A conservative judge is usually very cautious about expanding its meaning and is inclined to permit the states and the people to handle issues which are not clearly spelled out in the Constitution. The liberal judges believe it should be more loosely interpreted depending on what's going on in modern times. That's why in many cases, particularly involving social issues and you, one hundred per cent of the liberal judges vote together and the same with the conservative judges but in the opposite direction. This presents a real dilemma for all of us for if they all read the Constitution - which is not written in Russian and take an oath to enforce it - how can the judges consistently, and I mean consistently, differ?

Well, I believe it has to do with hormones and brain neurotransmitters which sometimes produce effects that are wonderful and sometimes not so wonderful causing all kinds of problems. I'm sure you know what I mean. Well, way back when the Civil Rights movement began the liberal Chief Justice of the Supreme Court said as part of his judicial philosophy that, in addition to the law, he would judge cases on "What's right". Now that's not an easy thing to do. And, as you guys know, "What's right" for one person is "What's wrong" for the next person, as exemplified by the abortion controversy.

The "What's Right" mentality on social issues means to the liberal Supreme Court members that, despite the Constitution and those great minds who framed it to protect us from too much government control, as I said before it is not good enough in modern times and that their personal feelings of doing "what's right" which also implies that they know "what's wrong" should be added to the Constitutional interpretation. One historic result is the establishment of the quota systems where you, as you well know, are denied such things as jobs and entrance in our universities. There have been recent court decisions that have gone against the quota system but they will not turn the tide for it is too firmly imbedded in our country's culture. No way, no how would our Founding Fathers agree that judges use their personal feelings of "What's Right" and "feeling good" as standards for decision making instead of more objective ones. It's like playing football or soccer without rules and referees. Anything goes and who knows where the heck it's going?

Thomas Jefferson said the purpose of law is to both create and limit the power of government. Evidently nobody is listening for government these days is just creating it. Government is now almost everywhere and getting ready to enter your bedroom both when it's not occupied and, you better believe it, occupied!

Speaking of Jefferson, his daughter once commented that she only saw him really smile one time. A friend of Isaac Newton said the same about him. I often wonder what it's like to lack a sense of humor. Or maybe they have it, but for some reason that has to do with their neurons and facial muscle interaction, they just can't express it with a smile.

Corporations

Except for the top-level managers in corporations who are predominantly white males, below them are employees that are part of a massive minority quota system. As mentioned before, males are disappearing from the ranks. The managers simply don't want to have long and burdensome battles with government regulators.

Media

I cannot emphasize enough that the media is overwhelmingly liberal. Anyone who denies it is like the Hindu friend of the Jesuit. But what is interesting is that conservative media has no problem admitting that they are conservatives while the liberal media makes a passionate effort to deny it. They fool you. Maybe it's because less than twenty-five per cent of Americans call themselves liberal, and if they realized that the media didn't share their values not only would they lose a lot of customers and lose advertising dollars but also lose credibility for masquerading and not being honest. There are some encouraging signs that Americans are beginning to catch on to what's going on which is very good news.

The vast majority of Washington national correspondents are liberal Democrats, and I would bet they are not churchgoers. Judging from what I see in the newspapers and television, imagine what they're thinking when they write about the Christian Conservative Right. Could they be objective and support their causes? Of course not! They would try in a subtle, unobvious way to hide their bias while undermining them. To tell the truth if I were a left liberal Democrat I would do the same. It's human nature.

And don't forget this: Generally speaking, the liberal media supports all the things that make a white male less competitive by trying to manipulate the mind of the people including you. It is not only women in the media who do this but also the girlymen.

Put this question in your head and try to answer it. "Why is there such a huge majority of left male liberals in the media and universities?" If you have a theory let me know for no one whom I know has answered this question that makes total sense.

What is interesting to note a relatively recent survey asked what professions the American people respect the most. Some of the results were as follows: The most respected was the military which the media don't respect; doctors were second and the Congress and the White House were at the bottom of the list while the media came in last.

Education versus Indoctrination

Our educational system, beginning with when kids are in diapers through our universities, like the media, is overwhelmingly liberal. It, like the media, tries to hide this and does a great job at it. These folks have helped whip the pants off the conservatives in the 2009 elections and deserve congratulations from a self-interest and competitive point of view. They view the world from a liberal perspective and that's that. And, if I were one of them, I would be very pleased with myself. The liberal faculties have taken over and now are so powerful that conservative voices, be they from the student body or university teachers, have a difficult time expressing conservative ideas and values. For example, let's look at two of our greatest universities: the law faculty of the first has only one conservative professor.

The others are liberal. Regarding the second one, during the last presidential election, those who contributed to the campaign all sent their contributions to President Obama, a liberal Democrat, and none to McCain, a Republican moderate. The same pattern of behavior holds for other universities.

Now get this into your head. Our educational system has become one of indoctrination generally promoting a liberal anti-you party line. This is both inevitable and understandable. It happens in all educational systems. But you should know it and not forget about it. Your parents, your uncles and aunts, your teachers, your female Cougars, your doctors, your lawyers and practically everybody else that's older than you have been and continue to be indoctrinated on liberal principles which emphasize equality over freedom and promote the necessity of all kinds of quota systems. So you can't blame all these people for believing what they believe in. The few conservative educators continue to be battered at teaching institutions. If they speak up, the majority liberal contingent launches counterattacks and almost always wins the competitive battle.

Another unobvious way that our educational system takes a hit at you is an indirect one because it understandably dramatically increases your effort to have orgasms which negatively distracts you and makes you less competitive. It's the way the gals dress. About ten years ago I was invited to speak to the entire school student body at a middle school- sixth, seventh and eighth grades. The principle, a nice guy, met me at the entrance and accompanied me to the auditorium. While we were having a little chat, a very attractive looking lady sporting a low cut décolletage approached him and asked to be introduced to me. After she left I asked the principal, "What grade does she teach?" he answered, "Grade? What grade? She's not a teacher. She's an eighth grade student." I said to him, "Who can concentrate on mathematics while sitting next to her in class. Not I." We both smiled and entered the auditorium. I ascended the stage, faced the audience and, there they were, gals to the center, left and to the right letting lots of what they have hang out. Now I have a weakness for attractive women, and the first thing that entered my mind was that I could never have made it to medical school surrounded by such "stimuli". I would have to go to an all boys' school or a school with a severe female dress code and no make-up allowed.

Now the "stimuli" become more stimulating as one climbs the age - maturity scale from high school to college. A few people told me that the boys become used to it and that I'm reacting like I was living in the old days when it was a thrill for guys to see a knee. I answered that there are now fewer and fewer virgins graduating from high school and that copulation and shacking-up is a way of life at our universities. Let me tell you that's not my idea of "getting used to it"! Later on I'll talk about the male orgasm and the bison that went bananas.

Now women know all about this male orgasm thing. One very bright, elderly, romantic and wise woman and friend whom I interviewed for this book said to me, "Steve, why waste all your time trying to write a convincing intellectual argument on the powerful driving forces behind the male orgasm?" She continued, "A joke or a poem or even a song can better tell a story and its message than a long novel." I challenged her to give me an example. She decided to tell a joke, and here it is:

"A mother was giving her four year old son a bath. When the bath was over and as she, on her knees, was drying the kid, he grabbed his penis and asked, "Mommy, is this my brain?" She, taken off guard, paused and then answered, "No. Not yet!"

DMS- The Demasculinization Syndrome

All these anti – you things going on I call the Demasculinization Syndrome or DMS. A syndrome in medicine is when a number of signs and symptoms occur in a particular condition. For example, there is the Pickwickian syndrome named after a very obese, man in Charles Dickens' *Pickwick Papers*. When a patient is extremely obese the fat in his body presses up against his lungs to such a degree that his capacity to breathe dramatically decreases, and he can't get enough oxygen in his blood. For this reason the body makes more red blood cells in search of more oxygen but fails to do so. When this happens he experiences somnolence which is a persistent and heavy sleep state. During my medical training, a bachelor Pickwickian who lived alone was found dead in his apartment. He fell out of bed but was so fat that he couldn't get up or even move to the telephone to call for help. What a way to die!

Now don't ask me to define the syndromes of masculinity or even femininity because they are beyond the power of words to describe. Words are best used for communication and not to define complex things such as love or happiness. Speaking of femininity, it was best described, in my opinion, in one word by the progressive female anthropologist, Margaret Mead. The word is "Receptivity".

Trying to define masculinity with words is virtually impossible. You, however, know it when you see it. Just watch a Clint Eastwood, John Wayne or Johnny Weissmuller Tarzan movie and you'll get a feel for it. If these examples are too way out for some of you, let's try Presidents Kennedy and Reagan. One wise woman suggested that the appropriate word to describe masculinity is "strength". But remember, words are best used for communication and not definition. For example, there are strong women and weak men and, by the way, what's the difference? Bottom line, it's like trying to define a horse's ass. It can't be done with words but you know one when you see one!

Let's examine some aspects of DMS starting out with bullying. Until recently, bullying mostly meant when a male made life both mentally and physically miserable to another male. When I was in elementary school I had to face two bullies at least a couple of times a week, sometimes on the same day. They weren't bad guys but just wanted to show that they were the kings of the hill. I managed to escape serious physical hits by using every trick in the evasion- of-danger part of my brain. There is no doubt that these experiences taught me a lot about survival in life which has served me very well. If you were to ask me now whether I would recommend that all young males face two bullies a couple of times a week in order to become stronger, I would leave that decision up to you. Despite what you are being taught today, let me tell you, adversity, disagreeable as it is, makes strong men stronger but the effect on the not so strong is unpredictable.

Modern day bullying is now a different thing. Changing the definition down to the point where it is including both boys and gals. PMS has joined DMS! The gal type of bullying is mostly verbal and their words are not, let's say, ain't lady-like. The guys are the ones that usually get caught in the act because it is mostly physical and, therefore, visible. If you even gently push someone, it is now considered bullying. But, it depends whose pushing whom. A high school senior told me that one day he was walking down a school hall with his sweetheart both being in a playful mood. They became touchy-touchy and pushed one another. A teacher, observing this, shrieked "Stop it! Stop the bullying!" The teenage lovers tried to explain to the teacher that they were just having fun but she would not accept that explanation. She then took them to the principal's office – and guess what? The male was accused of bullying and was then suspended. The female, despite her pleas that she also pushed him, was not suspended.

Another big but not fully appreciated implementation of DMS is the growing attack on anger for it is mostly aimed at you. The expression of emotional and physical anger is more characteristic of men than women. If anyone disagrees with this just tell them that adults in anger management courses and students in anger management classes are practically all males.

Anger is necessary for it is a powerful natural emotion force that drives us to take action to correct a wrong be it to an individual, group or country. It can happen in many ways. If someone robs and physically harms your mother, you would be angry as angry can be, help the police find the guy who did it to put him in jail. And if you had a chance before he was put behind bars, and if you could get away with it, you'd beat the crap out of him and be happy about it. I would. But in today's world the cops would put me in jail for assault. Since I come from a family of police officers, I know that they would not want to, but in today's world they have to. But get this; when I was young the police would have congratulated me. Imagine a policeman congratulating me today. If someone found out he'd lose his job. No one is immune from DMS!

You guys are too young to remember this. There was a candidate running for the President of the United States who was asked by a media guy during one of the televised presidential debates something like, "If someone murdered your wife would you ask for the death penalty?" He showed no emotion or anger and said he wouldn't.

Besides the fact that millions of Americans actually witnessed this on television, even though he was a liberal whom media loves, the media, though they didn't want to hurt their man, did report on this after the interview because it was a hot story which sells newspapers. Don't forget, media is a business like any other business and making bucks is their primary goal even if oftentimes the truth takes a hit. Remember, self-interest comes first. The result of this interview? His response played a major role in his defeat.

Let's take a step back in history. I hope you guys have been taught that Japanese bombed Pearl Harbor killing lots of our military personal and almost wiped out part of our naval fleet. This created a mighty wave of anger in our country that sparked our national determination to successfully defeat the enemy, including the Germans, in World War II.

Sure there's a destructive side to anger. The Roman Stoic, Seneca, called it "temporary madness". It's like most things in life - a double-edged sword. I'm sure many of you have been or are in love, and you know that sometimes it can be great and other times truly painful.

Before I move on I'd like to tell you about how the Italians handle anger. I first noticed this when I was young when family members would heatedly argue over some issue such as a perceived insult. The sparks flew, usually around the kitchen table and it was not uncommon to hear curses such as, "May God strike you down dead" or "May you end up and burn in Hell –forever"! To tell the truth, my friends, the language was oftentimes worded much more, let's say, strongly.

Now with most people insults and curses such as these would lead to a long break in their relationships, perhaps forever. Not with these folks. After a week or two, the tempers usually cool off and everything goes back to normal.

There is therapeutic aspect of this type of anger. We all have things pent up inside that cause what the Italians term *agita*. It's something like agitation but even more. You get it out of your system by blowing off steam. Try it sometimes but make sure it's with the right person!

As you probably by now are aware, I have a particularly strong feeling against the acceptability for people to squeal or snitch on others.

In my opinion men who squeal are not true men but demasculinized ones. Today, you and others are being encouraged to squeal. There is a powerful movie, *The Scent of a Woman*, starring Al Pacino in a very masculine role with all its weaknesses and strengths and a very good young actor that you must all see. It's about a student along with his buddy in a private school who saw other buddies commit an act of vandalism. They dropped some type of liquid on the school headmaster's car and they were big time pressured to squeal on the vandal students.

At the end of the movie there is a dramatic and moving scene at the school which occurs in the general assembly hall with all of the students and teachers of the school present. The headmaster apparently puts a lot of pressure on both of the students but no one knew that he made a deal with the father of one of the kids who was a wealthy contributor to the school and the kid did indirectly identify the vandals. Then the headmaster turns to the other kid, Pacino's friend, and really turns the heat on but the kid refuses to squeal. The headmaster then threatens to expel him from the school and that's when Pacino steps in and delivers a moving defense of how proud he was of his student friend not to snitch or squeal and that's what manhood is all about.

I won't tell you about the end of the story because I want you to see it.

I can go on and on about DMS and DMS-PMS but here's what happened when I interviewed two bright and pleasant female and male students that attend a high level university, that doesn't recognize, or let alone, celebrate Columbus Day - you know, Christopher Columbus, the guy that discovered America and the one big reason we are here. I truly enjoy being with young energetic and bright folks like these two. They challenge you. But let me also add, that I sometimes more enjoy being with a waiter, a carpenter and those people that have not attended super schools but live in the real world trying to earn a living and take care of their loved ones. It's a different hit. Unlike the students, they are experiencing life's real battles.

The young lady told me that a very dominant educational theme at the university is the necessity for a woman to be independent both economically and career wise. On further questioning, she admitted that the independent theme really was directly aimed at being independent from men. She also said that male students frequently agreed with this theme which is a reflection of the persuasive forces of the marketeer liberal educational system. Interestingly enough, male and female students who disagree with their professors remain silent but for different reasons. The guys don't care that much about debating the subject matter but also fear the possibility that they might offend the teacher and end up with lower grades if they spoke up. With the ladies it is a different story mainly based on fear. If they defend traditional values such as the family and stay-at-home mothers, they are aggressively criticized and even mocked by their pro-independent female colleagues. They also share the fear of the silent males that their marks would be not as high as they deserved. Now let's turn to my conversation with the male student.

Like his lady colleague, he was cordial and energetic with a fine mind. Somehow we stumbled on the topic of his history course and what happened during World War II. His professor taught him that the United States soldiers had little to do with winning the war. He told me that the Russian male soldiers were the greatest and it was Russia and not the United States that defeated Nazi Germany. There was a subtle anti-military and anti-U.S. tone in his voice.

Frankly speaking, I couldn't believe that a male professor had the balls to indoctrinate – and not educate – his eager-to-learn students and get away with it at any university. But then it dawned on me that I shouldn't have been surprised for it subtly represents the DMS that is now commonplace in the educational system with the support of the girlymen male faculty.

America Then And Now

"All Things Change"

Heraclitus

Y ou may be wondering more about where I'm really coming from and why I wrote this book. Those of you who saw the film, *Butch Cassidy and the Sundance Kid*, remember that Paul Newman and Robert Redford, two playful, outlaw cowboys, were being followed by a gang and they had no idea who they were. During the film, one of the two, I've forgotten which one, would periodically stop, turn around and, observing the gang in the distance, would ask, "Who are those guys?"

I was born at home in 1936 (a long time ago!) and over the years have witnessed the big time changes that have occurred over three generations both to you, your parents and everyone else. Though it's tough for most of you to believe, my father introduced me to philosophy when I was about twelve years old. My favorite philosopher was and remains Aristotle. One of his statements that had the most impact on my life was his advice to, "Observe, observe and observe". I bought one hundred per cent into this advice and ever since then I like to observe what's going on in all walks of life. One disturbing conclusion is that young men such as you are taking a huge negative hit all over the place and hardly anyone, from parents to schools and practically everyone else, understands what's going on, let alone is objecting to it. Whether you know it or not, you're in a world of fierce competition. Many of these forces are great and growing and working against you and you are losing out. So it makes a lot of good sense to try to recognize and handle them in order to set your sails in the right direction of life. Life ain't easy, my friends!

Now turn off your cell phones, Blackberry's and other stimuli, if you know what I mean, and try to imagine what it would be like to be me when I was young and how it would affect your feelings and thoughts of what's going on today not only as young men but also in general.

I was reared during the 1940's in an old Italian neighborhood in Philadelphia. Most of our parents were born in Italy and immigrated to our great country seeking opportunity. I was a first generation U.S. born Italian –American. There were six of us- my mother, father, grandmother, grandfather and brother, who lived in a very small row home on a city block of about fifty homes. After you walked through the front door, if you took ten steps you were out the back door.

There were about six or seven cars on our street, one owned by my father. We were one of the lucky ones! My world was confined to three city blocks. Going beyond that was an occasional and exciting adventure. We ate at home every night and, except for weddings and other rare family celebrations. I ate out at my first restaurant when I was seventeen years old. Every year we took a vacation to Atlantic City. My father, mother brother and I slept in a single room with two beds that was about four by six yards with only one window and no air conditioning. Let me tell you I remember well some very, very hot, sweaty nights. There was only one bathroom with one shower, no bathtub, and two toilets available to all the guests - about fifty of them.

Take a pause now and try to put yourself in my place. Think about it for a minute or two before you go on.

I was about twelve years old, at the same time I learned from Aristotle to observe, when we got our first telephone. It was, however, a "party" line, which meant it, was shared by two or three other homes. In the beginning, as you would do - Aristotle's advice or not - I had great fun carefully lifting the telephone receiver off the hook and listening in to my neighbor's conversations. Sometimes I didn't lift the receiver carefully enough and the other parties heard the click and knew that I was listening and gave me holy hell. It was fun at first but most of what I heard was so depressing that I decided to listen no more. But this experience taught me something that I would never forget. I must always try to be positive or else or I'll end up being miserable - which I hate and so should you. You know that there are lots of people that are happy being miserable. Go figure.

About a year after we got our first telephone, my father decided to buy a new technology product - a television. At that time about four or five families in the neighborhood had one. There were only three channels- can you conceive of this? My grandmother and grandfather couldn't speak English but they were fascinated by the television tube. I vividly remember that they loved to watch the so called professional wrestling matches, and I couldn't convince them that it was all entertainment and not for real. But they refused to believe it which taught me about how the mind wants to believe what it wants to believe- and don't forget this for we are all this way.

Regarding sports, there were no grass fields in the neighborhood. We played softball, stickball and touch football on asphalt streets or cement schoolyards. There was one basketball backboard in a schoolyard. We use to periodically tape the ends of the footballs because they would tear at the seams when they hit the cement or asphalt. There was no tennis, soccer, lacrosse or swimming. Oops, I almost forgot. There was a single public swimming pool about 3 yards wide and 6 yards long with about 100 kids in it at a time with no room to swim. You were only allowed in the pool for one hour at a time.

Regarding the young ladies, forget about it! They were not permitted on the streets by their parents except to go from one place to another. Mingling with the boys was a no-no and for good reason; they were a hungry lot, their bodies surging with hormones.

There were no pizza or fast food places that had chairs and tables where the guys and gals could hang out even if it was allowed. In addition, most of us didn't have the money to buy the stuff.

The ladies put on no or very little make-up, didn't own a tight sweater and wore skirts that ended below the knees. If the boys did get a quick look at a knee you can bet that at night in bed they didn't say their prayers but were thinking about other things.

In addition to the very strict social pressure against pre-marital sex, there were also no oral contraceptives available. Condoms were available but they were not nearly as reliable protectors as they are today. The risk of pregnancy was high and abortion was a big no-no not only because of neighborhood beliefs but also because the surgical procedures in those days carried a lot of risk for the woman. We knew that it occasionally occurred but rarely to whom. It was like the old Mafia's Omerta, the sworn oath of secrecy.

We knew of one case of abortion when somehow the news leaked out. Lizzy Lou was about 18 years old when some one out of the neighborhood impregnated her. Lizzy Lou was a class gal and everyone felt for her. One day she disappeared, and we never heard anything about her again. Though we weren't sure we believed that her folks sent her to live with her aunt and uncle in Rhode Island. We weren't sure whether the reason was to go on with the pregnancy or to have an abortion. But we all agreed that it was none of our business.

Marriage happened at young ages. I would estimate that about eighty per cent of men and ninety-five per cent of women had sex for the first time in their lives on their honeymoon. Less you forget, it has almost always been that way in all world cultures until modern times but it is still common in many countries, particularly for women.

Now this may come as a surprise even for women. Most of the households were controlled by the wives. A man would come home from work and hand over the paycheck to his wife. She would then give him his allowance for the week, and she was responsible for almost everything else making most of the major decisions. Even most of the strong men handed over their checks but they, however, played a major role in home management particularly in controlling the children. The women would routinely take a small percentage of the salary and deposit it in a savings account. The stock market was never even considered as an option. In a real sense, those women had more power than modern women which is today hardly mentioned and, therefore, not appreciated by you.

This may also surprise you: yes, there were a few wife beaters but there were also a few husband beaters. There was a guy we called Johnny the Pan because his wife, about once a week, would periodically beat him on the head with a fry pan. The poor guy almost always had bumps on his head.

We did have a double standard when it came to beatings. The wife beater was despised and considered an outsider - not one of the guys. If things got real bad, the neighbors would get together to try to solve the problem. But the guy whom the wife beat up was laughed at and no man felt sorry for him but, ironically, many women did. We had a hunch there were other man beaters in the neighborhood, but the beaten men were too chicken and embarrassed to let anyone know and the families kept it quiet in order to preserve the dignity of the beaten male.

Despite that you guys are being taught the opposite, well designed physical punishment or even the threat of it can oftentimes have a beneficial effect on bad behavior. I well remember Babs the Boozer. Babs was a happy drunk. Unfortunately, most drunks are hostile which makes for added pain to all those involved, particularly the family, for a long period of time. Well Babs had a strong-willed and muscular wife named Giuseppina. For some reason I remember her huge hands. One night she decided she had enough and hit Babs on the back with a rolling pin which is made of heavy wood and used to flatten out pasta dough. It probably fractured a couple of ribs. She threatened to beat him with the pin every time he came home drunk. But, being an alcoholic, he couldn't help it and came home again drunk as a skunk. She whacked him on the legs and back which made it difficult for him to walk. His body was increasingly covered with black and blue marks. This happened for about a week and the guy was whacked daily and in constant pain and could hardly walk. Babs decided to give up the booze for fear of his life. You may be thinking why he didn't call the police. That simply was not done in those days. Affairs of the family, unlike today, were private and none of anybody's business.

There were two elementary schools; one was Roman Catholic and the other a public one. Practically everyone in the neighborhood, almost all of Italian descent, went to the Catholic school. For some

39

reason my father sent me to the public one where, with a couple of exceptions, all lived outside of the sharp borders of one side of neighborhood. We are talking about a single street! Most of the students were Irish and German. There was one black lad, Henry Casey, who became my school friend. We both became teachers in the school dancing class. Some of you are probably thinking since Henry was black he was a better dancer than I. Not true. I was the best in the school!

The Catholic school students used to tell me stories about how strict the teaching nuns were. Discipline was enforced big time. There was no fooling around or your "you- know- what" got into deep "you-know-what". If you stepped out of the boundaries such things as having your hands really wacked with a heavy ruler or heavy detention penalties were common. Not infrequently, the kids were assigned to what they named the "nun's cleaning squad". For example, they had to get on their hands and knees to scrub the vestibule or entrance to the church or sweep all the floors of the school or clean all the windows until they were crystal clear. Now here's what interesting for you to think about. Despite this degree of discipline, the students rarely told or complained to their parents for one simple reason. It was useless! Unlike many of your parents today, those parents would with rare exceptions, such as loss of a finger, take the side of the nuns and even add to the punishment.

Believe it or not, though not as severe in dishing out punishment, the public school teachers were no different. Discipline was enforced mainly by the threat that the teachers would contact our parents directly, and they would react just like the parents of the Catholic school pupils.

Now here's an interesting story that happened with a somewhat different message: There was in our class a girl named Mary Ellen, who was a real snob. She was always dressed prim and proper and had a brief case filled with well-sharpened pencils, both colored and regular, writing pads and all the rest of the fancy school materials. Bobby Shay had a single stubby pencil, like most of us, which he periodically sharpened with a knife. I remember Mary Ellen well that day as she entered the classroom with her nose in the air putting on the airs like she was the Queen of Sheba. (Look up this fascinating queen in the Old Testament, that's the first part of the Bible, in your cyberspace world. Unfortunately, she's now not on Facebook or MySpace and also can't be twittered).

Well, one rainy day Bobby had enough of her baloney and decided to take action to bring her down to earth. In those days every classroom also had a cloakroom where the pupils would hang up their coats and jackets. He cornered her in the cloakroom out of sight of everyone and placed a big smacker- a kiss- on her lips. She pushed him aside, ran out to the classroom and squealed to the teacher. The teacher then told the principal who suspended him and told him she wanted to meet with Bobby and one or both of his parents before he could come back.

He told both parents about what had happened. His mother gave him gentle hell and his father smiled. After his mother left, his father said, "Son, don't tell anyone this, but I'm proud of what you did but the principal had no choice but to suspend you." Bobby told me his dad never said another word about it. They then both met the principal and he explained what had happened. Bobby's father gently whacked him on the back of the head and casually told him not to do it again. Bobby wasn't sure but he swore that the eyes of teacher and his father were quietly smiling. For your information, whacking on the head was a common practice in those days. It can be very effective to help keep the peace.

The important message of this story is that a parent handled the situation where his son came out okay and respect for the teacher was maintained. No screaming or legal threats or anger management, just old-fashioned polite behavior that worked.

At this point, I'd just like to put in a good word for teachers. Yes, today there's lots of justified controversy about our educational system but let me tell you that good teachers had a tremendous positive influence in my life and teachers today should be encouraged to do what has become the increasingly difficult job to inspire students to learn.

Pushing, shoving, fights, bullying and cussing each other out were common almost everyday events even on school grounds. You were usually on your own in these situations which, despite what you hear today, were effective learning experiences on how to handle tough situations in life and make you stronger. But there were neighborhood unwritten rules which put limits on the degree of physical and mental harm. Here are some examples:

One night at the weekly church dance, a nice guy called Bummy was dancing with a well-endowed attractive gal sporting a tight sweater who came from another neighborhood. Lou the Hammer noted for his famous big punch went over to Bummy and slapped him on the face in front of everybody, grabbed the lady's hand and started to dance with her. She looked back at Bummy with imploring eyes as if to say, "Save me. I want to be with you and not this animal." Much to our surprise, Bummy went over to them and told Lou that he wanted her back. This was a dangerous move with this guy, to say the least. Lou then, with a backhand, whacked him again. Bummy fell down, got up and tried to pull her away. Lou was about to finish him off with a right hand punch when a bunch of the guys pulled Lou away and told him in no uncertain terms to let Bummy alone with his honeybun. Lou then knew he had crossed the bridge of acceptable neighborhood rules and backed away.

Most of the time when there was a fight on school grounds, the teacher would break it up and depending on the amount of physical damage done, would make a decision whether to tell the parents or not. If the fight happened on the streets and was getting out of hand and the boys did not stop it, then a neighbor would step in and usually end it. And believe it or not, the neighbor was usually the manager woman of the house!

I vividly remember the day that Pretty Mo was getting his ass kicked in by a big guy whom, I can't remember his name, nobody liked. I can't even remember what started the fight. The guy was a bitter lad and bitterness was not tolerated by the boys. Who the heck needs it? Now Pretty Mo was not into physics or Shakespearean literature but was a dedicated full time student of meeting girls. He was the first and only guy in the neighborhood that used hair spray and a hair blower, and we used to kid him about his hair that stood up straight like a picket fence and moved very little when the wind blew. But the guys took a liking to him because he was an innocent creature floating somewhere in outer space. We used to wonder how may hours a day he spent in front of a mirror.

Now Pretty Mo was no match for the big bitter guy and was being beaten badly. Before the boys could step in to stop the slaughter a mother in a nearby house came running toward the two screaming with the vocal volume of a great operatic soprano, "Stop it, you hear me, stop it"! She actually tackled the bitter one, could you believe it?, trying to pull him off of Pretty Mo. The bitter one, with one strong arm, pushed her aside, and she fell to the hard cement ground where she hit her head and blood began to flow from a cut on her forehead.

This was a huge error of judgment for mothers were held in such high honor in the old neighborhood that this act was considered a mortal sin, the kind of sin that is considered unacceptable even to God. The boys pounced on him and were ready to teach him a lesson. But the mother, with lots of emotion, told them to leave him alone and the boys, of course, obeyed out of respect. She reprimanded both of the combatants and told them never to have this happen again. The case was closed and everybody left the battle scene. Today, the bitter boy's parents would probably sue the mother!

I can go on here with the many learning experiences that helped me understand what life is all about and how to handle it but I'll talk about some of them later on. But let me close by briefly telling you a few more facts. There were no hyperactive kids and no Ritalin. There was no marijuana, coke, meth-crystal or whatever. The kids were drug free. There were no counselors, therapists or special school classes offering psychological help to handle dealing with life. To be sure, life today is much more complicated and confusing and there is a reason why they now exist. But there is a huge unrecognized down side to this trend and we must begin to do something about it.

Now let's talk about being "THERE" or "in my shoes." A long time ago I learned that you oftentimes never know how you would react to a situation unless you are "THERE" and actually experience it. I, as a young man, have never been in "your" "THERE" living in your modern life. But, I am at least observing it first hand while you have never been "THERE" observing what happened in my life.

Let me give you an example of what I mean by being "THERE". When I was young I wondered how I would react when faced with death. Would I be a coward, boom-boom in my pants, cry and run away or would I be strong and confront the danger that could end my life? Well, I guess God wanted to help me out so he arranged for me to face a number of life- threatening encounters two of which I'll describe.

(Speaking of boom-boom, during the 16th and 17th centuries before commercial fertilizer was available, manure was used instead. It was frequently transported in large amounts on ships. It was in a dry form to lessen its weight. When water leaked to the bottom of the ship where the manure was stored, a fermentation process began the result being the release of a very flammable gas, methane. When a sailor went down to the hull to check things out with a lighted lantern there sometimes followed a huge explosion sometimes enough to destroy the entire ship. A smart guy finally figured out what happened and came up with a solution. Bundles of manure were now stacked up high enough in the hull out of water's reach with a label reading, "Ship High In Transit" or S.H.I.T. And thus the word was born and continues to be with us).

Getting back to death scenarios, the first happened in a dense mountain forest where I have a log cabin in bear territory. When I hike in the woods, I have a defense strategy in case I come across a threatening bear. I load my 38-caliber six-chamber pistol which was my father's when he was a policeman about 70 years ago. Not much of a lethal weapon particularly because I'm a lousy shooter. Anyway, I only load four chambers leaving two empty in case I fall while I'm climbing and the pistol goes off automatically and shoot myself in the leg. I put the other two bullets in my side pant pocket. Also, I carry two canisters of bear spray, one in my shirt pocket and one in my back pant one. If I met a potentially killer bear, I would slowly reach in my pocket, reach for the other two bullets and fully load the gun and place it in my right hand. I would reach for the spray in my shirt pocket and place it in my left hand. I keep the other canister in my pants pocket in case the bear gets to me and hopefully I would be able to reach it during the brief struggle and spray the face.

One afternoon as I was descending from a mountain I saw a little black poodle running around in the woods about one hundred yards away. I looked for its master but saw no one. Then I saw a second little poodle but still no master. As I approached the poodles I heard a rustling in the bushes and, lo and behold, there appeared the mother bear about ten yards from me. If that ain't a life threatening situation, my friends, nothing is! I then realized that the poodles indeed were not poodles.

Now was clearly the time I should have gone into action with my bear defense strategy. Right? Wrong! I didn't reach for my bullets or my canister but, instead, simply raised my arm and pointed the pistol toward the heavens and instinctively, without any reason, stupidly decided to stare the bear down. Now let me give some advice. If you ever come face to face with a bear, never try to stare the creature down. You'll never win!

During the entire encounter which lasted for about sixty seconds three thoughts came to mind. The first, the mother bear's face resembled that of my close medical doctor friend, Joseph DiPalma, the former Dean of Hahnemann Medical College. The second, if I killed the mother bear, her cubs would die. The third, to hell with the cubs, my life came first!

Needless to say, the bear won the staring contest. I blinked first. I turned around and slowly walked away from the bear with my pistol still pointing towards the heavens. Then I remembered that from a starting position, the bear is faster than a racehorse for a short distance and thought that the creature might be speedily coming my way. I turned around again and the bear was still staring at me. I then, without any reasoning behind it, spontaneously shouted with full throttled vocal cords, "Boo!" This did the job. The mother bear lurched backwards, turned around and raced toward her cubs. They all then vanished into the woods. I decided, for the sake of adventure, to follow them but, after second thoughts, wisely decided not to press my luck.

During this sixty second encounter I felt no fear either during or after. My heart did not pound, and my adrenalin levels stayed normal.

Another encounter with death occurred when I was in the then beautiful city of Beirut in Lebanon. I was having lunch at the historic St. George Hotel, which has since been destroyed. I heard both gunfire and bombs exploding nearby. I decided to get out of town in a hurry. I packed my clothes, hailed a cab and took off to the airport.

On the way there we came across a tank on the same side of the road facing us. The tank turret turned and pointed its cannon at the cab. The first thought that immediately came to mind was, "What a goddamn stupid way to die - in a foreign country by a tank bomb. It makes no sense." Instead of being afraid, which would be the normal thing to do, I was mightily pissed off. I told the cab driver, who understood English, to stop the car for I wanted to get out and talk to the people inside the tank and tell them that I was an American. He advised me not to do this, but I rejected his advice, got out of the cab, walked right up to the front of the tank, pulled out my passport and shouted, "I'm an American and I'm going to the airport." I repeated this three or four times and then stood still facing the turret of the tank. Nothing happened. I went back to the cab and told the driver to go around the tank and take me to the airport. And so he did without any interference from the tank people.

What was interesting, as with the mamma bear, I never felt any fear. On the other hand, if I didn't have the pistol and bear spray, it would have been a different story and my boots would have been shaking! The same if the guy in the tank got out, shot the cab driver in the head and escorted me to the tank.

Do you remember the very scary movie *Jaws* where this giant killer shark was constantly looking to eat people? Well, I saw it five times. The fifth time was on a flight to Europe. I was sick and tired of the movie but I was not in the mood to read so I watched it without turning on the sound. Would you believe it, and I can't tell you why, that it was scarier than the other times I saw it. After I arrived at the majestic Hotel Hassler in Rome, I was afraid to get into the bathtub!

(Just for your information, the actual size of Jaws is about a yard or so long and in a museum somewhere. Film technology made it seem like a giant).

The point I'm trying to make is "THERE" means actually living the moments of life which is different than not being "THERE". But, being an actual observer like me of modern times, it can help bring an objective point of view to the table.

You were not "THERE" in my old neighborhood but try to imagine yourself in a restricted environment with no television, radio, computers, cell phones, ladies, sex, restaurants and money and few barriers to being a natural boy which is essential to becoming a man. Then place yourself as an objective observer with the power to see what's going on today and try to make a comparison. And then go on to the rest of the book.

And remember this: Though I can't prove it, there is little doubt in my mind that the kids in my neighborhood were not only happier than today's kids but also grew up and became better men.

What is Right and What is Wrong?

What is Moral and What is Ethical?

"For there is nothing either good or bad, but thinking makes it so."

Shakespeare

After waking up, all of us are heavily bombarded by messages from all kinds of people and groups. As I said before, I call them marketeers or hidden persuaders pushing their self-interests which includes media, government, business, educators, bloggers, entertainment industry, religious groups, you name it, all trying to influence and control our minds. Subjects cover just about everything ranging from what color and style of underwear you should buy and wear on your dates on liberation Saturday nights to the morality of euthanasia (or helping a person who wants to die before he or she normally would). And recently cyberspace has enormously increased- more than you know- the power of these already powerful marketeers to manipulate your minds and control your thinking and your personal lives which eventually impacts what happens to the strength of our country. And I'm sure that the nighttime dreams of most of you have been affected in many, let's say, interesting ways. It's time to wake up!

Much of the information that's fed into to your minds is pure baloney and what is interesting is that a high percentage of the marketeers that feed you this baloney actually believe in the baloney themselves. Many of them seek fame and fortune and are having an ego trip in successfully achieving these goals. And I bet that you, as well as everyone else, are either confused or don't have the slightest clue what's going on. So turn on your concentration powers to read this chapter more than you normally would for if you don't know where you are or don't know where you're going, it can make you wake up in the morning looking forward to the day or wanting to stay in the sack all day long. You must be aware of the forces around you. Just take my word for it.

I'm not taking a negative shot at you for not being aware what's going on. As normal human beings, we develop routines which make decision making easier. We get up in the morning and get on with our lives of eating, work, reading magazines and newspapers, communicating in cyberspace, trying to handle problems with friends and family, trying to make or get enough money to maintain our level of living among many other things. If you think about it, your life is filled with a ton of detailed things, and I often wonder how the human brain handles them all. You simply don't have time to try or want to reason in detail what you should do in every situation. Try to imagine what it would be like just to objectively analyze what you read in the newspapers or computers- you'd go nuts in about an hour. For example, should we have invaded Iraq?

An already huge and rapidly expanding market is the powerful market of behavior controlling ideas where the marketeers are trying to tell us what is right or wrong particularly what is moral and ethical. They are pushing religion and tradition aside affecting almost every aspect of our lives and country. Believe me, it's revolutionary and never experienced before. Many of these value judgments are based on the use of just crap reasoning with heavy emotional overtones. So you better get the hang of the game not only to protect yourself but to get good daily laughs instead of the kind of agitation that confuses which makes you lose in the competition of life.

The ideal way to really know whether something is true or not involves what philosophers call "universals" and "epistemology".

(Don't put the book down! Hang in there!). Universals represent the absolute truth. For example, is there such as thing a pure dog? There are over four hundred breeds of dogs of different shapes, sizes and mental behavior. There must be a universal standard or actual pure dog on which we judge other animals to be dogs for how can we call a dog a dog unless there is a standard one? If there were no standards then why can't we call a cat a dog?

Now enters epistemology: Even if we make the assumption that there is a universal dog, how, in God's name, can we know and specifically define it? Philosophers have tried to use reason to discover not only what the universal dog is but also where it exists. Why don't you give it a try?

Let's now go on to a higher level and deal with the issue of love between a man and a woman. The universalist philosopher must first try to define it before the epistemologist tries to find out what it actually is when put in action. Your first instinct would be that certainly it exists for that's the stuff of man-woman relationships in every day life since they both got together after the Big Bang. Books, poems, love letters and the intimate experience of couples throughout the ages certainly support its universal existence and the epistemologists should have no trouble defining it. Right? Not so! And why is that? I would suggest, if you're old enough share a glass of wine with your honeybun and discuss it. It will be more enlightening exercise than reading all the literature on the subject. But before you do this, finish reading this chapter.

Basically, there are two ways to clearly know whether something is true or not. Either God tells us or by the use of reason. There's another way which is not as precise but takes us closer to the truth which I'll talk about later on.

Now let's not mess around and instead go directly at the heart of the matter and confront the universalist and epistemological questions that are immensely and negatively affecting your lives, "What is morality and what is ethics and how should we apply them in our lives?" I want to reemphasize that you must read this carefully for moralists and ethicists of all types are riding high affecting much of everyone's lives.

Morality deals with general principles of good behavior. For example, "Do not tell a lie" is a general principle that parents begin to teach their kids early in the game. The ethicists take this general principle and apply it to real life situations. Let's say parents with limited income cheat on their income taxes – which is telling a lie- to have enough money in order to send their child to vocational school or college. This would be considered an unethical act by the professional ethicist but to normal hard working people it would be an understandable and good, i.e., an ethical, act. Whose side would you take? If a rich man, however, cheats on his taxes that would be clearly considered unethical. Or would it since the government wastes his money?

Now here's a tough one regarding the moral principle, "Do not rape a lady": Mike Tyson, the former heavyweight champion of the world, met a young lady college student somewhere and asked her to his room. She agreed and went with him where he then allegedly raped her and broke the law. He was convicted and spent time in jail. Apart from the law, this act of rape was deemed an unethical one by practically everyone except the old ladies of my old neighborhood. I met about a dozen of them at a delightful Italian dinner reunion one night in Philadelphia. The ladies were in good form. They ate their pasta and drank a little wine. It was a happy group until the subject of Mike Tyson's rape came up. How it did, I don't remember. Anyway the mood of the ladies suddenly changed. One of them, obviously a little bit angry, and I still remember the exact words, shouted out, "What the hell was she doing in his room anyway? Did she expect him to ask her whether she knew how to make goddamn meatballs and what was her goddamn recipe?" The group agreed, without exception, that she should have known better. Tyson is a rough guy with tough upbringing and that sex drives men to rape under certain circumstances. In other words she invited the rape and was the blame and not poor Mike who was like a hungry bee chasing, pardon the pun, his honey. In other words, the ladies invoke another moral principle, "A woman should not tempt a man to rape because of the powerful natural force for a man to have an orgasm". She broke the moral code and committed an unethical act by going to his room. It is interesting to note that, to my knowledge, no one publically offered a similar balanced opinion which says a lot about our times and the power of the marketeers creating anti-you values.

Using the reasoning of the old gals, whose side are you on regarding this moral-ethical issue? Would men and women disagree on this? If so, why so? Think about this because here's an example where emotional reasoning pays a huge role in peoples' views. Try talking to people about politics and religion, and you'll know what I mean by emotional reasoning.

Now we have another dilemma: The conflict of moral-ethical standards for the individual person versus the country is a hot issue, and will be increasingly so in modern times. As I'm writing this book there's an ongoing debate that deals with torture. The moral operating moral principle in our country is "Thou shalt not torture". So if you torture someone just for the fun of it or to find out where he hid his wallet by the use of repeated electric shocks, then the act is considered unethical. On the other hand, suppose you were a CIA agent and captured a terrorist who knew the 9/11 plan and how it would be executed before it happened and used the same repeated electric shock treatment and the guy spilled the beans and three thousand lives were saved. Would you consider torture in this case an unethical act? Is the safety of our country and three thousand lives more important than torturing a single or even a number of terrorists? What's your decision?

The discussion of the previous examples was purposely brief. But now let's examine in greater detail the complex morality and ethics of the emotional issue of abortion. You can be sure that few will be happy with what I have to say even though I do not offer a personal opinion.

The law hasn't declared an unborn fetus a person. In fact, I'm not sure what "it" is. If, therefore, you terminate its life, it is not legally an act of murder. But here we are not talking about law but about the morality-ethics positions of those with opposing views- pro-life (anti-abortion) and pro-choice (pro-abortion). The former consider abortion as an act of murder while the latter does not.

I believe that most in either group accept the universal, moral code, "Thou shall not kill." Applying this to abortion, the pro-choice reasoning is very clear. The fetus is not a person and, therefore, no violation of this universal moral-ethical code is made by the pregnant woman or the doctor by the act of voluntary abortion. An additional moral-ethical argument is that a woman has a right to her body which makes it ethically acceptable to have an abortion. But they do not tell us where this right came from. Certainly God, to my knowledge, did not give an opinion on this subject and certainly reason cannot take us to this conclusion. Furthermore, I haven't been able to find a definition of what this right entails.

A few years ago I met the medical director of the emergency room at a Manhattan hospital. One night a pregnant woman was taken to the hospital because of an overdose of heroin. When she was lucid the doctor told her that heroin puts the baby's health and even life in jeopardy. She shouted something like, "This is my body and I have a right to it. Anyway, I probably will get an abortion later on."

The truth is that women only have this right because the United States Supreme Court decided that they should have it. It is a legal right. It wasn't so before the Court's decision and will not be so if the Court reverses it which, though remote, is a possibility. To repeat, we only have rights where we live at a particular time which can be taken away later on. Once upon a time cowboys had the right to carry their loaded pistols into bars. Those days as well as those rights are now history.

Getting back to abortion, here's another issue that understandably greatly adds to the confusion. It's partial abortion which is when the act of abortion is done in the late stages of pregnancy. Let's look at a dramatic case to clearly see the point where a pregnant woman who is in labor suddenly decides, for whatever reason, she doesn't want the baby and asks for and undergoes a legally permissible partial abortion.

There are lots of pro-choice advocates that really are turned off from this procedure for though it is indeed a brutal one, the fetus is still a non-person both legally and within their moral-ethical standards. Nothing has changed. The procedure involves the doctor inserting a probe into the brain and sucking its contents out and then crushing the skull with a forceps so that the fetus can more easily be extracted from the uterus. I'm not a mind reader but in this case there's an important lesson to be learned about why there is a oftentimes a change of heart by the pro-choice people. It's a complex issue, to be sure. After all, the potential child is fully formed and almost "THERE" sometimes a couple of inches away before entering the vaginal canal unlike a tiny one month embryo. To add to the confusion, where and why they would draw the partial abortion line-one week before when labor is expected, one month, two months or the day after or before three months.

Over the years the majority of folks who are pro-choice, including friends I met and with whom I discussed the abortion issue, are against partial abortion.

Now let's take a look at what the pro-life folks have to say about abortion. Their position is simple and much less complicated on making judgments but equally flawed based on lacking a firm foundation on the universal truth, morality-ethical basis. Though some fuzzy heads may deny it, their position is impossible to deny. The fetus is a "potential" human being and if anyone denies that send him immediately to a psychiatrist. The disagreement between the two is that the fetus should be treated as an actual person. To abort the potential human being, they claim, is the same as murdering anyone that has already been born. Now to my knowledge God has not spoken out against abortion nor can reason take me to the conclusion that the fetus falls under the same moral-ethical umbrella as a person.

Though some of you may think I'm being a wise guy playing around with logical games, I'm not. I'm simply trying to deal with the complexities of those marketeers attempting to force a false system of universal, moral-ethical truths that are having an enormous negative impact on not only your life but on almost everyone else's.

What about history and other countries? How did they handle abortion and unwanted children? Well, safe abortion techniques were not available until very recently so people usually waited until after the baby was born then killed the newborn either soon afterwards or within the first year or so. This type of act is called infanticide which is considered murder and unethical in our country.

Infanticide was very common in all kinds of countries from the poorest to the richest of folks regardless of the cultural differences. The reasons were many ranging from attempts to limit the population or to using people as sacrificial lambs to the gods or simply because the parents either didn't want them or could not afford to feed them.

Before I go on, you probably are unaware of how common it was to sacrifice humans to appease the gods. Here's an example that even I, who accepts the fact of man's inhumanity to man, find it difficult to conceive. It, however, tells us a lot about how big and common it was and about human nature.

The people of the great Aztec civilization believed that it was a sun god that created their civilization. They feared, however, that if they didn't show their appreciation in a big way, the sun god would become angry and destroy the Aztecs. So they decided to sacrifice human beings as a way to please him. Now use your imagination here: the priests decided to, as a way to kill the sacrificial human, cut their hearts out while they were living like it happened to the poor soul in Kafka's novel, *The Trial.* There was a scene in one of Indiana Jones movies where this ritual was simulated. The sacrificial ritual took place in a huge room, I believe in one of the Mexican pyramids, where the "volunteers" lost their hearts- and I'm not talking about to their sweethearts. If you looked outside of this room one could see two lines of people to be sacrificed extending for about two miles! We are talking about thousands of people. I sometimes wonder what I would have seen and heard if I were present in that room and how I would have reacted. Just for the record: I would not have been the brave one and tried to stop the slaughter for I value my heart very, very much and don't give a damn about the sun god.

Getting back to infanticide, most of the time it was the female baby who was the victim for reasons such as they were not strong enough to do what men do such as working the fields to produce food or fighting the battle against enemy warriors to protect their families and their territories.

In China they would submerge the unwanted one into a bucket of cold water. You wonder who thought of that. In Japan the *mabiki* technique was used where they would put wet paper over the mouth and nose of the babies. How could they watch? The Romans, in order to avoid too much guilt - that's my opinion - were a bit more sophisticated and civilized about it. They used an indirect technique. Rather than kill the babies themselves, they would "expose" them which means they would drop the kids off somewhere such as the local garbage dump where they would be unattended and eventually fade away. Oftentimes, however, the babies were "saved" by the less rich Roman families to be reared as slaves.

What about the animal kingdom? This is not the place to go into detail but both abortion and infanticide take place. The latter occurs most frequently in animals such as lions, particularly by dominant young males who kick the old-timer dominant male out or even kill him and then take over the harem. He then kills the kid of the old-timer male and even sometimes the female participates, so she and he can start a new family and spread his genes.

But, if you are not paying attention, you may be wondering how abortion can occur in the animal kingdom where there are not abortionist doctors. In the tiger shark, for example, while two or more fetuses are in the embryonic phase waiting to be born, the stronger one frequently eats the weaker one.

Does religion help out in finding universal truths on abortion? Certainly God gave Moses the Ten Commandments one of them commanding, "Thou shalt not kill". But there was an awful lot of justified killing in the Old Testament. Just ask the Egyptians about the Exodus! In practically every culture from the primitive to the sophisticated there is always a war god or other gods that not only justify but also encourage killing particularly those folks in competitive countries.

There are other examples of justified killing such as a soldier killing enemy soldiers in order to defend himself and his country and an individual killing an assailant in self-defense.

What's critical for you to understand is that the unfounded moral – ethical principles are being applied to the smallest of human acts such as the use of foul language and what you eat. Someone who works with Congress, a very serious chap with an absent sense of humor, recently told me that there was now consideration of making cursing a hate crime because it is "immoral".

But here's one example in my medical world that I'm not sure whether I should laugh or cry about. It deals with the moral – ethical issue regarding how cadavers are treated in medical schools. For example, a student posted on Facebook a photo of another student posing next to a cadaver with thumbs up. This, would you believe, has led to a movement to create moral – ethical standards on visual representations of cadavers. Now, if the student did not have his thumbs up but just stood next to the cadaver then there wouldn't be a problem. Do you catch the absurdity?

Once more, in the past it was very common and acceptable for medical students to take photos with their cadavers in all kinds of ways.

Let there be no doubt that the micromanagement of your behavior is moving forward full steam ahead.

In conclusion, there are no universal truths that support any immutable moral-ethical standards. Only God, as President George Washington said in his farewell speech to Congress, can give us these standards. But God does not play a role these days. In fact, he is prohibited in modern America to be even mentioned in schools and other public places. What was moral-ethical in the past is not so today and will oftentimes revert back in the future. In a real sense, history does repeat itself. Is this a cause for pessimism? Yes and no. Yes, because your minds are increasingly being bombarded by moral-ethical messages that are simply false and misleading and you are big victims of it. Briefly put, you're being brainwashed. No, because there are ways to handle this which I'll discuss later on.

But before we get to these issues let's talk about God and religion and keep an open mind for it's important.

God and Religion

"If God didn't exist, it would be necessary to invent him."

Voltaire

Because of your age group and surging hormones, this chapter will probably hold the least interest for the overwhelming majority of you. But pay attention for religion has always been with us, in one form or another, and has an enormous influence on individual lives as well as the course of nations and history. Today, religion and God are under almost fanatical attack from a lot of influential people and groups. Few realize what a heavy unnecessary, negative hit it's having on you and everyone else including the attackers themselves.

Let me clearly state my position up front: religion can be a tremendous and necessary force not only to help someone handle the constant problems of life but also to keep our country strong. Many who disagree with me haven't honestly thought it out or do not have the brains to do so. Most of the times, unfortunately, it's due to emotional hang-ups and brainwashing from the marketeers.

Let's first ask the complicated question, "What is religion?" There are many definitions but as far as you are concerned living here in the good old United States a working definition is, "Religion deals with the relationship between man and a personal God and a personal afterlife such as a happy heaven and a hellish hell." The description of each varies. But, in each case, the good folks go to heaven and the bad ones usually go to hell either for a short time or forever. Traditionally, our religion is based on the teachings of Christianity and Judaism but there is now the growing influence of Islam which also embraces the existence of a personal God and an afterlife. In addition, modern surveys reveal a growing pagan trend of mysticism such as spiritual energy that is being embraced by even orthodox Christians.

Why do so many believe in a personal God as well as an afterlife? The prevailing belief is that people created God to have someone who is all-powerful to turn to if they have problems and also because of their fear of death. There is little doubt that religion particularly thrives when there are certain threatening problems in life. For example, if a loved one, such as a mother or father, is doomed to die because of a fatal disease, many pray to God for help to cure the parent or at least lessen their pain. During wartime people flock to their churches they had previously abandoned to pray to God for the survival of their loved ones as well as themselves. After 9/11 the churches were filled but, after the passage of time memories of fear faded and the churches were empty again because there were no additional attacks.

The atheists use the following argument to support their position: Since modern technology has gotten rid of plagues that wiped out humungous percentages of populations, since food is now abundant and starvation is not a threat, since medicine offers therapies to treat many diseases and since the United States has not had a war fought on its soil for a long time, people feel less a need for God, and the churches are now empty. The belief in an afterlife has diminished. And they are correct in this observation. Technology tends to undermine religion.

Then they, adding on to this argument, are effectively spreading the message that religion acting in the name of God is a major cause of war. Much to my surprise even some of my even- minded pretty intelligent friends have been fooled and buy this false argument. Let me tell you that it's absolute baloney.

War is natural to man, and it will always be that way. Wars are nations' ways of eating. It's in their nature! Throughout history wars have been fought for the main reason of gaining power. Some leaders use religion as an *excuse* to kill and conquer and others do not. In the past one hundred years the greatest numbers of people have been killed during wars than in any previous century. Hitler in Germany, Stalin in Russia and Mao Tse Tung in China killed tens of millions of people without religious reasons. In fact, the greatest killer nations, Russia and China, were atheistic states!

Getting back to the attacks on religion, they are happening in a number of ways. The bad news is that parents and organizations, with certain exceptions, are taking a back seat. The attacks come from our universities, courts, liberal organizations and media- formidable marketeer forces that direct and influence your and mostly everyone else's thinking. I spoke to a very religious student at a major university who, one day in class, was asked by his teacher about his religious beliefs. I believe he was a Baptist. He said he was a Christian and believed in Jesus Christ. Silence then followed as if everyone in the room thought he was a weirdo. He told me he decided to keep his religion to himself at the university

Look, you can't prove that God exists by any objective or scientific method. It is not like two plus two equals four. So where does that leave us – in purgatory? Yes and no. For centuries philosophers and theologians have come up with some interesting arguments to support the existence of a personal God and an afterlife but they are not scientifically objective. We must try to put together pieces of a puzzle that will convince us of at least the possibility. One interesting puzzle is composed by three big pieces and many little ones that make them up.

The first deals with St. Anselm's Ontological Argument. He was a theologian who lived about a thousand years ago. He believed that since God is a being whom nothing greater can be thought of and since the human mind is limited and cannot go beyond these limits on its own, God must have put it there. Do you follow it? Think about it.

The second deals with DNA and RNA and, yes, my favorite philosopher, Aristotle. The relation between these molecules is not clear. Everyone talks about DNA as "the" molecule but evidence now exists that about 3.5 billion years ago, RNA was the first form of life. But let's stick with DNA for that's the current "in" word. Guys, this may be getting too heavy for your concentration span and Facebook, Twitter and cell phone messages are, like an attractive woman, beckoning you to take an easy intellectual route and cast aside the hard stuff. My dad often reminded me not to be like water and take the path of least resistance which is downhill.

Speaking of women, the British poet Leigh Hunt wrote, "The two divinest things this world has got – a lovely woman in a rural spot".

Getting back to DNA, Aristotle asked the question, "What makes a thing what it is? What makes a chair a chair and what makes you-you?" He called that force, "Entelechy". Well, I asked myself the question, "What makes DNA what it is?" DNA creates all forms of life from the single cell bacterium to the human body and mind and that mind, by the way, thinks about God. Science hasn't the slightest idea why. There's something in this genetic material that makes DNA do what it does and it is not unreasonable to assume that there may be some type of intelligent design or entelechy behind this whether it's God or some other kind of guiding force.

There's the third piece, a powerful mystery, which cynics sneer at and the religious embrace. It's called faith in God and his teachings. It's a one hundred percent belief without a shred of doubt. God gave us the Ten Commandments and you better live by them or you're in trouble. Jesus said, "Love thy neighbor as thyself" and if you don't, the inference is that you'll burn in hell. Faith makes decision- making in life easy. There's nothing like God backing you up!

Now I'd like to tell you about my encounter with faith for I was "THERE". I learned some invaluable lessons of life that I would not have learned or appreciated otherwise.

You remember that practically all the guys in my neighborhood went to Catholic school and were practically indoctrinated not only with the messages of the Bible but with the Catholic Church as being the true Church that Jesus Christ established. Jesus said to his number one disciple, Peter, "Peter, you are a rock and upon this rock I will build my Church." The interpretation is that Peter was the first pope and all the following popes are connected to him. The guys learned about what is good and what is evil, about good behavior and Heaven and Hell in their Catholic upbringing.

Now don't ask me why because I don't have the answer. I was always curious to learn about the Catholic religion, and when I was in my third year of college I decided to find out. Little did I know that I was off to a beautiful adventure with God which somehow sadly ended during my second year in medical school.

I took night and summer classes in philosophy, theology, logic and other courses mostly at the famous Jesuit college in Philadelphia, St. Joseph's. In those days, glory be to God! , it was an all male school which, believe it or not, I much prefer and so should you. Can you believe that?

What surprised me at first was the attempt of the Church to use reason and not emotional hype to support its teachings. I, being curious for reasons to believe in God, was very much impressed and encouraged by this. Indeed, the famous Irish playwright and atheist, George Bernard Shaw, once said that Catholicism is the most rationale of all religions. In fact, he had a nun friend in a cloistered monastery where the nuns were not allowed to leave but only communicated to their family and friends through a thick screen that separated them. The romantic side of Mr. Shaw was expressed by his comment that he envied the spiritual freedom that she had in her confined religious, God-oriented life, the freedom that he lacked.

But after reading and thinking about the rationale or reasoning arguments of the great Catholic, and, yes, non-Catholic religious writings, I realized that this did not bring me any closer to God. Sure, I understood and appreciated their intellectual positions but I became really discouraged for it did not give me the faith, the powerful convincing belief not based on science, to communicate and be close to Him. (Notice, I capitalized Him which drives modernist, anti-religious folks crazy, and they don't know why. I do).

Then I decided to read the works of the mystics and other religious people, mostly Catholic such as St. Francis of Assisi and Theresa di Avila who were overwhelmingly in love with God without the use of reason. In other words, they had the thing called faith where reason can't take you. What was common were two things- prayer and talking to God which you may think are the same, but they are not.

Now here's what happened to me, and I cannot explain why. It just happened! I started to pray and talk to God and then faith arrived in full force. I was absolutely convinced that there is a personal God and a personal afterlife. It's difficult to put in words how things went but I'll give it a try. Then use your imaginations to try and put yourself "THERE" with me.

Let me first start on some details. The Catholic Church teaches that there are three persons in God- the Father, Son and Holy Spirit or what is called the Trinity. It's a complicated story but the believers either pray directly to God or Jesus believing that they are both the same. I never met anyone that prayed to the Holy Spirit. Now I prayed to both God and Jesus, and I haven't the slightest idea why, on each occasion, I chose to pray to one and not the other. Many Catholics also pray to Mary, the mother of Jesus, to ask her help to get their messages across to Jesus. Don't get cynical for there is a beauty in this custom. It helps lots of people, and we all need help!

I tried to pray to Mary but I just could not connect and, to tell the truth, I was disappointed. Today there is a huge push from the Catholic Church to have its members pray directly to Mary. It is probably due to the powerful and beautiful concept of traditional motherhood.

I prayed and talked to God every day. I read heavily about Christianity both Catholic and Protestant. I attended the Catholic Mass as often as I could preferring the quietness of the way the Mass was in those days to the noisy one of today which detracts one's from going to a higher spiritual level with God.

How did I feel with my rendezvous with God? There was no religious high; no swoons or rushes of adrenalin which, to tell the truth, I would not mind experiencing. I can't say that I was happy for I haven't the slightest idea what happiness is. I just felt calm, confident and strong. It reinforced what my parents had already taught me and permanently stamped it in my mind such as don't think of yourself too much, help others as much as reasonable, don't think about material things too much, keep your word and be independent.

After classes I worked at various jobs, and at night, after I finished my studies, I frequently would go to a local bar- somehow I looked older than I was- have a couple of beers, observe and listen to the customers talk about their problems among other things. I would do some of my best writing there (and still do!). Sitting on a bar stool is a great learning experience. It's like being with a great teacher. One of my secret desires was to be a bartender and learn, first hand, what goes on in the minds of all types of people. Booze does indeed loosen the tongue and now and then makes a temporary honest person.

Ladies did not play much part of my life at that time, and maybe that also helped me stay on course!

Now here's the mystery which still puzzles me. My relationship with God slowly faded away. There was no defining, critical moment. I did meet a young lady and maybe this had something to do with it. I don't think so but I can't be sure. Maybe in my next book about women, I'll tell you why we broke up.

So God left my life and, regrettably He has never come back. Now and then I do try to reconnect but it hasn't yet worked. But I haven't given up hope. I would strongly recommend, despite your current hormonal state of mind and what the marketeers are feeding you, to think about or at least give it a try sometimes in your life. You cannot have faith unless you want and will it. There's nothing to lose and much to gain provided, of course, that you connect with the right God! It's called Pascal's Wager.

Before we go on, I'd like to tell you of an experience that I had when I was primarius or president of the medical student fraternity Phi Alpha Sigma at Jefferson Medical College which happened after I lost my faith. At that time, though the fraternity had real financial problems, I managed to raise enough money from our alumni to keep the two cooks in the kitchen so that my medical student colleagues could be together at breakfast, lunch and dinner to talk about medicine, politics and other things. Interestingly enough, I recall few conversations about women and none on the subject of making money. Times have changed indeed!

It was a unique fraternity for it was not an ethnic or Ivy League type but was composed of a mixture of Catholic, Jew and Protestant males some of whom were religious and others not. Once in a while I would raise a topic for discussion at dinner. At that time the national controversy over abortion had begun. I asked my colleagues to speak up and be open about their opinions emphasizing that they be logical about them. Surprisingly enough, the discussion was not heated. There were the pro and anti-abortionist as well as the "I don't knows". None, however, could adequately support their arguments using reason. We all threw up our hands in surrender.

I then thought how much more easy life would be if most of our population had a single religious belief –be it for or against- an issue like abortion. It just would be accepted without much controversy. Religion right or wrong, just makes it easier.

And if someone today asks me about my current belief in God, I would answer with what the old world, romantic philosopher, Santayana was supposed to have said, "There is no God, but Mary is his mother."

What's Life Really About?

"Before you enter the jungle, make sure you know what size animal you are."

Rudyard Kipling

I'm not sure what you have been told about life but whatever it was, let me tell you it ain't a bowl of cherries. Whoever tells you that he or she is happy either has mental problems or is eating some laced peanut butter cookies purchased at a Grateful Dead concert.

Before I go on, let's take a look what some famous, successful and experienced personalities have to say about life:

"Life is meaningless." Ecclesiastes - the Old Testament

"You are born, you suffer and you die." Joseph Conrad - famous author in the past

"Life is one damned horrid grind." Charles Dickens - one of most famous novelists of all time

"You fall out of your mother's womb; you crawl across open country under fire, and drop into your grave." Quentin Crisp - author

"You are born and you don't know why. You are here and you don't know why. You go, you die. People suffer." Woody Allen - actor and comedian

"Life is a tale told by an idiot, full of sound and fury, signifying nothing." William Shakespeare - perhaps the greatest playwright of all time

"It's a very short trip. While alive, live!" Malcolm Forbes - was a famous successful businessman

"The true object of all human life is play." G.K. Chesterton - very entertaining author and philosopher

"We make a living by what we get, but we make a life by what we give." Winston Churchill - great English leader during World War II

"Love life, above everything in the world...love it, regardless of logic as you say, it must be regardless of logic, and it's only then one will understand the meaning of it." Dostoevsky – Russian novelist and profound thinker

"We must free ourselves to be filled by God." Mother Theresa - was a famous Catholic nun

"Life on earth is only a preparation for the eternal home, which is far more important than the short pleasures that seduce us here." Muhammad Ali- great world heavyweight champion

"Christians affirm that God, the all-powerful creator of the universe, became a man in the person of Jesus Christ. He taught that God is love, and that He is willing to forgive us when we commit our lives to Him. He offered us hope of an eternal heaven. I believe that He is the answer to every individual's search for meaning." Billy Graham - was the most popular evangelist of modern times

As you can see, there is a broad spectrum of opinions but no one, to my knowledge, has shown that not only are we made to be happy but here's how to successfully find it. (W.C. Fields, a comedian from way back said, "Smile first thing in the morning. Get it over with!").

So where does that leave you? Well, let me tell you: Life is a rough and tough battle with no definite answers. It's competitive from your personal life to national politics, never quite right and we are always searching for more than we currently have including peace of mind. St. Augustine, the great Catholic theologian wrote, "We are restless oh God until we rest in Thee".

You may find this weird, depending on your definition of weird, but when I was a teenager- and it continues to today- I often wondered what life is all about, including the possibility of an afterlife. Though I don't remember the exact words in the Catholic Catechism, a religious instructional very small book for the faithful, it asks some of the following questions among others: "Why was I born? Who am I? Where am I going?"

I read a lot and also spend lots of time on my favorite and most educational pastime, observing and listening to other people. I would highly recommend that you develop this habit for it can be, as I said before, one of your best teachers in life. I would put it at the top of the list along with some others.

I made certain conclusions or judgments, some of which I was not so sure of, but then something happened that strongly supported my thinking. It was the emergence of highly sophisticated photojournalism and documentaries which tells it as it is because it is real life in action and not just opinions expressed in words with no factual basis. It's like someone trying to verbally describe what happened at a rock concert versus actually being there. There's an old saying that a picture is worth a thousand words. I say that it's about a million; on second thought, impossible fully to describe!

Armed with their high tech cameras these guys visually record what really goes on in life from what happens from the formation of the embryo, how ants build and live in their ant hills to how the lion kills its prey to feed the lion pride. (Lions live in groups, the pride and new born live with it and are not left alone. Cheetahs are loners. The mother leaves the male cheetah and raises their kids to a certain point and then just walks away. Is that familiar to some of you?).

Before I go on, here are some of the interesting things that I learned watching the animal videos: Hummingbirds flap their wings 100 times per second and honeybees a 1000. Elephants defecate about 220 pounds of feces each day and along with it release enough methane gas to move a car for 20 miles. Newborn kangaroos are the size of a pea. The blue whale was the biggest mammal ever weighing 174 tons (348,000 pounds!) and made sounds louder than a rocket launch. The giraffe has the same number of cervical vertebras that we have and sleeps less than an hour a day. A hippopotamus farts through its mouth. Wolves' sounds do not echo and cows kill more people than sharks. (I would check some of these out, particularly the kangaroo one, for I usually watch these videos after a couple of drinks).

Now to some of the major characteristics of the animal kingdom that we share with them: They kill just to kill, kill to eat, have sex, rest, sleep and, most importantly, their leaders exercise power to control either individuals or groups. The photojournalists show us ways in which a wide variety of meat- eating animals seek and kill other animals working in groups or alone and then feed on them either alone or sharing with others. It's a rare person who prefers to watch bears eating berries instead of watching a scene where bears attack and kill an aging or injured deer. (Wouldn't it be interesting to see a mountain gorilla fight a bear)? Think about these things for they say a lot about us.

Much goes on in these videos that send messages about us. For example, in certain species you see the young heartily involved in play but play then fades away with the passing of time. I personally love play for there's something in it that's uplifting to the spirit of living but I haven't the slightest idea why. How about you? Though I don't know what it's all about, I fear the day when I lose my interest to play which signals that it's the end of the line. Don't forget, play doesn't have to be physical. Humor is in my mind the best way to play. Here's an exercise for you. Try to define humor or what makes you smile or laugh like someone who inadvertently farts at the dinner table.

And now we come to, you said it, sex. Before we go on, let me say sex, in the right doses and the right places, is a wonderful thing. The videos don't tell us exactly when sexual mating occurs. Is it after a meal and rest or before or in between? Does it depend on the species or type of animal? Whatever the case let me tell you that sex is a big time motivator, and many times in a downer way, of much that happens in your life and the world. It is bigger in our country than ever in any part of the world. And it's getting stronger and creating more problems that far exceed periodic moments of pleasure. Animals go wild to mate to have offspring. They even kill their mates as part of the act. The female preying mantis bits off the head of the male during sex act and, though it is tough to believe, the male speeds up his performance. Though I know of no human female that's bitten off the head of a male during the sexual act, during these times where freedom to do what you want is becoming common, I would strongly advise you to beware of making love to women with physically big mouths! (Pardon me, ladies, I couldn't resist putting this in).

Because of sex's extreme importance in affecting human behavior and its powerful and growing influence on the road you take in life, I've devoted the following chapter to this subject.

If you were to ask me what the core or basic message of the animal kingdom is that relates to human behavior I would say the exercise of power and survival. Both include competition, sex, dominance and strong leaders as well as other characteristics. (There are exceptions, however, for example, animals don't cook).

Darwinism, which is very much talked about these days, holds to this view. Darwin, by the way, was a very religious Christian, a fact that is purposely rarely mentioned by his nonreligious marketeers of his theory.

Let's now go to the highest animal in the animal kingdom - man. It is obvious that we share the exact same characteristics with animals but carry them to a much higher, complicated, selfish and cruel level because of our more developed brain. Animals don't hide the fact that they kill another animal while humans are expert at trying to avoid being caught after they commit murder.

Rather than make a list of all the destructive things that human beings do to each other, I'd like you to use your own brains and those of your friends and answer this question. "What would happen if all laws both in the United States and the rest of the world", and I mean "all", were abruptly abolished? Do me a favor and visit cyberspace and ask your friends the question and ask them to answer them and then get back to me with the results at www.DoctorDeFelice.com. Let me tell you it will be learning experience that you and your friends will never forget if you hang in there and really think about the question.

You will then understand why humans, unlike animals, have a legal system and courts mainly to protect their asses.

There are four subjects that I'll now talk about that you should have a general understanding of because they are and will be with you and affect your lives in a big way until you are buried or cremated or blown up. They are war, socialism, capitalism and equality versus freedom. They may not be as interesting as the topic of sex but concentrate on these issues for they might help you handle your life, including how you vote, in these rapidly changing and confusing times. Just take my word for it, and if someone tells you otherwise, put on your earphones and listen to 50 Cent or Beethoven and shut him or her out.

War

Now let's talk about war for we are in the age of nuclear, biological and cyberspace warfare weapons and God knows what other kinds. It is and will remain the most important and immediate and long-term danger that we face but the headlines are instead filled with other topics such as economic and health care ones. We are like ostriches with heads in the sand. To repeat, war is a nation's way of eating which means it must be constantly fed. In all of recorded history there are only a couple of hundred years when no war is mentioned but I believe it's because there were no pencils, pens or papers in the countries where they were fought or the historians were murdered and their writings destroyed.

Wars, always driven by leaders, are based on competition, domination and power to conquer and destroy or control another nation or a civil war where battles are fought in the same nation. It involves the same principles as when you try to get a girlfriend by competing to take her away from her boyfriend. Somebody wants to get what somebody wants. It's as simple as that, and don't let anyone with a fuzzy head tell you otherwise.

Most of you have never experienced war, but let me tell you, pray to God, that things will stay this way. There are massive killing, cities destroyed, torture of the real kind, rape and everything else that brings about cruelty and suffering on a massive scale.

I don't know what history courses you've been exposed to but you should by now know something about Alexander the Great (a Greek) and Julius Caesar (a Roman). These two legendary leaders conquered practically any country that they wanted to. After killing many of the males and sometimes destroying entire cities, they would take the women and children back home as slaves. History is loaded with other leaders of countries who conquered and slaughtered other people such as Genghis Khan and Attila the Hun. (The country, Hungary, was named after the Huns).

During the last one hundred years alone, there have been umpteen wars ranging from local ones to two World Wars, and they are still going on as you are reading this book. Tens of millions of people have been killed, crippled and God knows how many mentally damaged.

Try to imagine when almost every day and night bombers are flying over your city dropping big bombs that kill and maim family members and neighbors as well as destroying all kinds of buildings and where there's blood all over. Try to put yourself in a scene where your neighbor's home was destroyed and everyone killed except your best buddy who is wounded and you find him crying, bleeding and buried under the hot rubble of his collapsed home next to his mom and dad who are crushed to death. Yes, you see these scenes on videos but you're not "THERE" which makes a big difference in your appreciation of war.

About twenty years ago, I had dinner in Rome with an Italian old-timer who was a very successful businessman. He told me a story that I'll never forget. During World War II the Nazis had stationed a large number of troops in Italy to make sure the Italians would not break from them and join the American soldiers in the battles for liberation. The Italians formed a group of rebels called the Resistance whose mission was to weaken the Nazi forces by ambushes, sabotages or whatever so that the American troops could more easily and quickly defeat them. Unfortunately, the local Italian citizens had to pay a price. For example, if the Resistance fighters sabotaged a bridge, the local citizens in the area of the bridge would take a big hit. In order to find out who did it, the Germans would kill a male, not a female - you know, the sex thing - in the piazza or public square where everyone could see. Sometimes a citizen a day was murdered until someone in the village spilled the beans about who done it. Occasionally it worked but, interestingly most of the times it didn't. Of course the number of killings was limited. My friend, smiled broadly for the only time that night. He said that if they killed all the men there would be no one to make the wine that the German troops loved. Interestingly enough he said that there were a few troops that were very friendly and tried to help.

Anyway, at that time my friend was a teenager and because he could keep his mouth shut better than the others he was selected by the Resistance to deliver messages to the Resistance fighters regarding what the Germans were up to in the occupied areas. This would help them plan their guerilla tactics. They decided to communicate with each other by handwritten messages which my friend would deliver on his bicycle. The messages from the village were written in the Catholic Church. Usually during the Catholic Mass my friend would receive the message and tuck it inside his shirt. Afterwards, he would get on his bike and ride out right pass the Nazi soldiers to deliver it. The guerillas would read it and then respond on a handwritten note. My friend would then bicycle back to the church like an innocent religious kid, pass the Nazi network of soldiers and give it to the village organizer who would then deliver it to the Resistance guerillas.

One day a German soldier did stop and frisked him. Boy, did he sweat bullets! He told me, "*Mi sono caccato sotto!*" which means I shat in my pants. He had a message tucked in his belt right above his rear end. The soldier, while frisking him, missed the note and his life was spared by about a couple of inches. Little things in life oftentimes mean a lot.

He told me about half a dozen of other war stories about man's inhumanity to man. There was one torture technique which he described in detail which made it difficult for me to continue to eat my pasta – and that takes a lot! The Nazis would place a hot iron through both eyes if someone wouldn't talk after which, if he continued to remain silent, they would cut out most of his tongue. What really amazed me is that this total torture technique was applied to two or three villagers who managed not to squeal.

There is something about the bravery of these men that puzzles me. It's almost something mystical, kind of a higher level of human behavior found in some area of the brain. I don't know about you but I'm not sure my brain has this area in it and whether I could remain silent as the hot pokers approached my eyes let alone thinking about losing my tongue. How would you react? A small detail: the tongue is a very vascular organ and when cut lots of blood comes pouring out enough to maybe put you into fatal shock. As a curious physician I asked my friend how they stopped the bleeding. He said they just did it with clean rags where the villagers took turns putting pressure on the hemorrhaging wound for a long time of what remained of the tongue.

Interestingly enough, the eyeless and half tongueless men survived and managed to live lives that were okay enough with the help of the villagers.

At the end of the dinner we were drinking grappa, an Italian cognac, and not saying much because we were both thinking about the heavy price of war. I'll never forget this truly powerful moment: He sipped on his grappa and suddenly with a deep voice that had the authority of God behind it said, "Stefano. Stefano, No more wars No more wars!"

(In case you don't know it, Stefano is my first name in Italian).

One final note: The Nazi war machine is the one most frequently referred to describing war's cruelties but just let me tell you there are those that surpass the numbers of people that were killed, crippled and atrocities committed in other wars. The lesson, once more, is that war is everywhere, and it won't stop until everyone on earth takes a happiness pill every day. And with today's technology this is a definite possibility. Now ask yourself these questions: Are you for it? Would you take the pill though it robs you of the natural forces of your mind including free will? For your information this possibility is now in the thinking phase of some influential, power-seeking folks. And, before I forget, wars will keep coming and don't believe otherwise so we better be up to it.

Socialism versus Capitalism

Socialism or the Left means that a government controls most of what goes on in your lives from taxes to education to health care and to the amount of water in your toilet bowl! It also places lots of rules on businesses which have a negative affect on making profits and hiring people. Capitalism or the Right is just the opposite. It's for less government and more freedom for both people and businesses. It relies heavily on leaving businesses alone to make money and by so doing they need to hire people and stimulate the economy. Our country is now a mixture of both.

The Founding Fathers of our country brought about a vibrant capitalistic country which made our country a great. As in any system, there were some excesses and the government oftentimes made good adjustments. Today, however, the government has apparently forgotten about the Constitution and is rapidly pushing us towards socialism. One of our great founding fathers, Thomas Jefferson, warned us that government is always pushing to increase its power too much. He, along with Benjamin Franklin and others believed that the Constitution permitted the government to create the proper amount of power while not letting it get out of hand.

In the United States a battle between the two is currently going on and will immensely affect your lives. For your information, the current Democratic Party is heavily tilted toward socialism while the Republican Party moderately toward capitalism. Increasingly, however, the distinction between the two is blurred particularly during the past ten years with Republicans going in the direction of the Democrats. At this point, it appears that the Republican party may be returning to its conservative and capitalistic roots.

Freedom versus Equality

Now here's something you should be taught early in your education for it's true and plays a huge role in the behavior of countries and individuals including your lives! The problem is that if your teacher taught this truth she would be first fired and then tortured by sticking hot needles under her toes until she repented and retracted her statement.

No matter what you have heard or been taught, freedom and equality are eternal enemies and they shall never shake hands. People are not born equal and with the same degree of freedom. The more freedom in a country the less equality and the more equality the less freedom. During the last few decades the United States has dramatically turned to legal enforcement of equality and freedom has taken a big hit for practically everyone. There is no doubt, however, you have taken the biggest hit – by far!

It's useful to compare the United States and The Soviet Union on these two issues. They are two great nations that took opposite tracks in their forms of government. The Soviet Union took the communist path of equality for all where the government took care of everyone from the cradle to the grave or as someone once said, "from erection to resurrection", in every detail of their lives including businessmen. Freedom was no where to be seen. The Soviet Union crumbled and is now history.

The United States took a daring freedom pathway from the beginning and became one of, if not, the greatest nation in world history. People flocked to our shores, and still do, while the Soviet Union had border guards all over the place to prevent people from leaving and settling in other countries.

Let me give you a real life story of what happens when the government has heavy control over many aspects of people's lives. I had a friend who was born in Russia during the Communist era. When he was a young man, he and his family, with the help of bribes to Communist officials, managed to escape from Russia and immigrate to the United States. He worked hard and became president of a large successful U.S. company. Like the Italian I talked about, he was a strong man and good guy. I like this combination in men.

One day I received a call from him asking me to be his consultant to help out with a big problem. I thought the problem was hopeless and was inclined to turn down the offer. But his vocal body language was warm and so persuasive that I couldn't turn him down. (For the record, we resolved the problem, and that was a happy day. It's nice to have happy days but they rarely come unless you make an effort to find them).

Besides being very bright, he was, more importantly a gentlemen and a man of his word, which I value high on the scale of masculinity. We quickly became friends which lasted a long time.

(Before I forget, there was a very talented and successful movie actor, Richard Burton, who married Elizabeth Taylor, who was one of the most beautiful and sought after actresses of the time. He had bought her a ring with a diamond that I believe was the largest one of its kind. One night he was interviewed by David Frost, one of the best interviewers at that time, who asked Burton, "How does a man capture a woman's heart". Without hesitation Burton answered, "Buy her a diamond". Now here's my point: though we know that women generally love jewelry there is another thing that, I think, is much more important than a diamond provided you know how to do it. I'll touch on this subject later on).

One night while we had a couple of drinks before dinner, my old friend, which was very uncharacteristic of him because he was a very private man, wandered down memory lane and told me some stories of his personal youth in Russia. Later that night on my way home I tried to put myself in his place. Like with the bear and the tank, I don't know how I would have reacted because I've never been "THERE". And here we go again: I want you to seriously think about this and how you would react for it is, as I indicated before, already coming your way.

There were communist government officials everywhere ordering ordinary people and businesses to follow their exact orders which came from the national headquarter bureaucrats. Who should work at what jobs and what companies should produce at what prices were the rules which is the opposite of our free market economy where the individuals decide their own destinies.

This was Communism's way to compete with the United States capitalism philosophy. History has proven us the winner-by far! But here's the scary part: these officials, armed with almost absolute authority were instructed to enter and control local communities and the families that lived there *which is the natural last phase of socialism.*

Example number one: In order to prevent the people from revolting, the authorities instituted a policy of spying and squealing. If you didn't answer their questions about the doings of your family and neighbors, you'd be put into prison with no time limits as well as undergo physical punishment. So it became natural for folks to not only squeal on their neighbors but, would you believe, on their mothers and fathers as well as the rest of the family!

Example number two: Government bureaucrats often decided they wanted to live in the best homes. My friend's father previously had a good business and could afford to buy a nice home for his family. One day a government bureaucrat decided that he wanted that home for himself and his family and ordered my friend's family to leave after which the comrade official took occupancy. He then kicked another family out of a much smaller home for his other family members to move into. The government guy then ordered others in the community to serve, though not officially, as servants.

Example number three: Here we go again- it's sex! If a woman was attractive enough the government official would request her periodic presence in his bedroom. If the wife and husband fought against this, the husband would suffer big problems including jail imprisonment. Of course, the wife and husband almost always gave in for there was no place to turn to. The courts were ruled by the government.

Over the years I have made a number of acquaintances with people who lived in communist countries who have confirmed this type of abusive government behavior. It's important for you to note that one main successful mechanism to achieve control over people was, by using fear tactics, to force them to squeal on others including, as I said before, their families! Guys, is it beginning to sound familiar?

The Scorpion and the Frog

You may be wondering why in God's name is life this way - selfishness, cheating, cruelty and killing among the many other things that don't exist in heaven. And, despite what you're taught that's the way the world is. It will never change unless, as I said before, the population of the entire world takes a daily happiness-be-nice pill. So be a Darwinian and adapt to reality or you'll lose in life.

After 9/11 when the Twin Towers in Manhattan were destroyed taking with them thousands of Americans lives, I met a young lady who had lost her fiancée that day. She, really full of passion and with tears rolling down her cheeks, said something like, "Why are people so cruel? Why are there wars? Why do people kill and murder? My fiancé was a kind man who wouldn't hurt a fly." And then she naively added, "Why can't people just sit down and talk to each other to iron out their differences and live in peace?" I was about to try to answer these questions but I couldn't for the truth would have made things worse for her.

There's a famous book, *Aesop's Fables*, mainly about animal stories such as The Tortoise and the Hare and the Boy Who Cried Wolf that carry messages and lessons about what life's all about. It was written about 600 B.C. by the Greek slave, Aesop. If you haven't heard about these fables then there's something wrong with your school curriculum and you should have changed schools when you had a chance.

Anyway, there's one story about a scorpion and an innocent frog. One day, as the frog was sitting on the bank of a large pond getting ready to cross over to the other side, a scorpion approached him and asked, "Mr. Frog, can you give me a lift to the other side? It's kind of a long way for me to travel around the pond. Plus, I'm very light and you won't even feel my weight." The frog, surprised by this request that could end in his own death answered, "Mr. Scorpion, do you think I'm some kind of idiot. You just want to sting and kill me and fill your belly with my blood and whatever else you scorpions eat."

The scorpion then gave what seemed to be a logical answer, "Listen frog, do you think I'm suicidal or am on drugs? If I sting you while we're crossing the pond, not only will you die but so will I because, and you know this, scorpions can't swim!"

The frog paused, thought a bit and then said, "You know, what you said makes a hell of a lot of sense. Hop on my back my comrade of the animal kingdom, and I will be a good neighbor and will safely carry you to the other side of the pond."

Well the scorpion hopped on his back and off they went to the other side of the pond making small talk along the way. And would you believe this? Half way across the pond the scorpion stung the frog and injected his fatal venom into his blood stream.

The innocent frog was flabbergasted. He couldn't believe it and said, "Why the hell did you do this? What are you, some kind of pervert? You can't swim and you know I won't be able to go back or make it to the other side of the pond before I sink and you will die along with me. You're just as nuts as those crazy people who blow themselves up. And, you brainless one, do you know what else really pisses me off?"

Before the scorpion could answer the frog said, "The reason why I wanted to cross the pond is because there's a beautiful and hot, young lady frog that fell in love with me the other day and is waiting for me there to begin our romance."

After that burst of adrenalin, the poor frog suddenly felt his energy going bye-bye and knew the end was near. Strangely enough, his anger left him and curiosity took its place. As he began to sink he spoke his final words in life and asked, "Mr. Scorpion, why did you sting me knowing that both of us would die"?

The scorpion was taken by surprise by this question and didn't have a quick answer at his fingertips for no one had ever asked him this type of question before.

The scorpion paused, thought a bit and let out a kind of frustrating sigh and answered, "BECAUSE, MR. FROG, IT'S IN MY NATURE".

And guys, this is the answer to the 9/11 lady's and anyone else's questions. It's the way human beings are and never forget it!

Now you may understandably think that I'm a pessimist and believe that we are similar beasts and behave like animals one hundred per cent.

Maybe I have mental abnormalities but, with very few exceptions in my life- maybe thirty days, I wake up each morning looking forward to my day and I like it that way. As the late Bishop Sheen said in a book that I read when I was a very young man, "Life is worth living." I couldn't agree more! I'll give you some of my thoughts on this later.

The Power Of The Orgasm

*"Sex is like fire. It can warm up
your home or burn it down!"*

Stephen L. DeFelice

If you didn't know this before, know it now: Sex has always had a powerful destructive, vicious side to it which is very common. Today you are living in an era of sexual liberation and there's more of it than ever bringing more destructive moments in young men's lives than ever. There are more homes burning down these days than warming up. *As I said before, excess pursuit of the orgasm takes your mind off your self-interest and makes you much less competitive.* So it is in your best interest to understand what this driving force does to you in order to handle it better. (Please don't ask me what my credentials are on this subject)!

(Points of information and interest: The human male erection is the largest in the primate kingdom. The average length of an erection is 5.5 inches whereas that of the largest gorilla is about 4 inches. The average time for a man to ejaculate is about 4 minutes while that of a gorilla is about one minute. I wonder if this means human ladies have more fun than gorilla ladies).

I'm sure what you've read and been taught about the forces that move human behavior and history are nowhere close to the way I see it. Bottom line, it's primarily about males trying to have an orgasm. It often carries with it unhappy consequences. Have you ever heard of Romeo and Juliet? Taking away all the romantic fluff Romeo's intent was not to have tea with Juliet but he was dying to hit the sack with her. And he killed himself in his failed attempt.

Ah! I know many are you are thinking that women have orgasms too. That is correct but it's only one part of the seductive arsenal that nature gave them to entice men to perform the sexual act and have their orgasms. Lipstick, tight dresses and subtle eye foreplay exist for certain reasons.

I want you to know that I'm not trying to be clever or a wise guy and upset lots of folks. I, as a physician and scientist, after spending *mucho* years on planet earth, have observed human behavior over three generations and have made certain conclusions. Sex is more powerful than we realize, and I believe it's having a tremendously negative impact on all of us except for pimps, ladies of the night and the porn industry where business is booming. The latter is estimated to be larger than the sports industry.

Getting back to the animal kingdom, you do remember how the big, female preying mantis bites off the head of the much smaller male during the sexual act. And let's not forget the poor male lion. When the female is in heat and ready, her sexual appetite is insatiable. It is estimated that she has hundreds of orgasms over a couple of days. During that time the male, mightily enjoying himself in the beginning, must service her calling upon all of his body's energy reserves. I am sure many of them croak from heart attacks either during or after the act and the females know it. That's why there are fewer male lions than females!

There was one television segment that I saw about a bull bison's preparatory ritual to find his honeybun mate that convincingly told the story about the male's uncontrollable nature-driven need to have an orgasm. For about three months before the act, the bison's sexual hormones begin to flow but instead of seeking out his honeybun he goes after and attacks his potential rivals for the lady bison. Over this period of time he fights and sometimes kills his competitor or is killed himself. Battle worn, he finally enters the herd to seek his mate. After having found her, he mounts her and within fifteen seconds he releases his sperm, has an orgasm and then walks away forever. (For the record, many human women know about this type of male behavior).

Three months of life threatening battles for a fifteen second sexual act and orgasm: That, my friends, should leave no doubt in our minds about the power of the orgasm. Another thing: I'm happy as hell I'm not a bison!

Before I move on, there's another example where the ability of an animal to have an orgasm is connected to an act of mental as well as physical sexual cruelty. It has to do with the male elephant. As I'm sure you know, elephants live in a herd or whatever you call it. There's the *numero uno* alpha bull male that is the leader. Nobody fools around with this guy unless a younger bull tries to take over. Under him are bull elephants at various levels of power that have sexual privileges. Numero Uno and his lieutenants have the pick of the gals when comes acceptance time. When the lady elephant is ready for foreplay, she shakes her rear end, wags her tail and the boys then do what comes naturally. But the younger male elephants just stand there and watch. I don't think elephants masturbate but some animals do.

It is only when a lesser bull elephant is about forty years old that he loses his virginity and has his first orgasm. There is indeed a cruel side to sex, both mentally and physically.

But what about we humans? Before we take a look at modern sex, let's take a walk down history's lane of sex regarding the penis and orgasms in one way or another. It's everywhere!

In the Book of Genesis of the Old Testament, it's the first part of the Bible-guys!, sex rears it's ugly, pardon the pun, head. God commands the naked Adam and Eve - the only lucky people, by the way, who ever lived who never had in-laws- that they could do anything they wanted in the Garden of Eden but could not eat the forbidden fruit of the tree of knowledge of good and evil. For centuries people believed it was an actual fruit. Milton, the English poet, effectively pushed the idea that it was an apple. At that time his great work, *Paradise Lost*, sold more copies in England than the Bible.

Now in the garden there was a serpent that really was the Devil. He (or was it a she?) convinced Eve to partake of the forbidden fruit and she, in turn, convinced poor Adam. They then became aware of their nakedness and were ashamed of themselves. When God visited them they covered their genitals with fig leaves. If it was an actual fruit or an apple they had eaten, they would have covered their mouths with the leaves! Do you get what I mean?

In Genesis other sexual events happen. The first was polygamy. Lamech married two women, Adah and Zillah. (Lamech was an amateur compared to other men. In the past there was a guy in China who had one hundred and thirty-one wives. Now get this; by law he was obligated to make love at least once a year to each one of them. In today's America, there's a heroic man who has six wives, forty-six children and two hundred and thirty-nine grandchildren)!

Other topics are sodomy and homosexuality where God destroys Sodom and Gomorrah because the men indulged in practicing sodomy with other men. God sent Lot, a good guy that lived in Sodom, a male angel to get him out of town before the catastrophe. The men of Sodom heard about this male and wanted him for their pleasure. Lot, would you believe, then offered his daughters to them but they refused. Lot had no choice but to get out of town in a hurry before God destroyed the city and all of its inhabitants.

Another deals with surrogate motherhood. Abraham's wife, Sarah, was supposedly too old to become pregnant and so he made love to their slave Hagar who bore him the son, Ishmael who plays a large role in current Muslim religious beliefs. (I am told that in the Koran Mary, the mother of Jesus, is the only female mentioned).

Jumping ahead to another chapter in the Old Testament, Deuteronomy, there are a number of sexual warnings against orgasms such as:

"Cursed is the man who sleeps with his father's wife…"

"Cursed is the man who has sexual relationships with an animal."

"Cursed is the man who sleeps with his sister…"

"Cursed is the man who sleeps with his mother-in-law."

What is interesting is that women are not cursed if they sleep with their fathers, brothers, father-in-laws and/or animals which I can't figure out. On the other hand, in this chapter women do take a hit in a strange way. It reads, "If two men are fighting and the wife of one of them comes to rescue her husband from his assailant, and reaches out and seizes him by his genitals you shall cut off her hand. Show her no pity." Go figure!

What is also interesting is that it is the penis and not the clitoris nor the vagina that has attracted all the attention in history including modern times of liberated sex which is a testament to the driving power of the quest for male orgasms.

Before we go on to sex in modern America, do you remember when I wrote that war is a nation's way of eating, and we will always have them because it's in our nature? I hope I'm right but I think I do have a way to stop wars and prevent the ultimate war that will destroy the earth. You guessed it. It has to do with orgasms.

Aristophanes, one of the great Greek ancient playwrights, wrote the play, *Lysistrata*. In the play Lysistrata proposes that the way to stop wars is for women to withhold sex from men until they lay down their arms. I disagree. In fact, I believe it would have the opposite effect. The guys, like tigers sometimes do, would go crazy and go on a killing spree. I would recommend that women take their men to bed 24/7, and you know what that will do to men's energy levels! Who wants to make war after making love?

On the other hand, I'm having second thoughts. Boccaccio is one of Italy's greatest writers who lived during the Renaissance and wrote the book, *Decameron*. In it a group of people that were fleeing from the plague, in order to amuse themselves, tell some humorous stories one of which involves a hermit monk, Rustico, and a virgin teenager, Alibech, who is seeking God.

There were a number of religious hermit monks who lived alone in the wilderness depriving their bodies of pleasure in order to free their minds so they could communicate with God through prayer. Rustico was one of them.

Alibech decided that the best way to find God was to visit these religious monks and seek their wisdom. She was a blossoming, young and sensual lady and, because of this, the wise monks, when beholding her, sent her away because of the powerful, sexual temptation they feared and did not want in order to remain close to God without any disturbances. Then one day she stumbled upon the hut of the young, virile monk, Rustico.

Unlike the others, Rustico, with hormones surging, happily invited Alibech into his hut. As she was explaining to him the reason for her mission she noticed a bulge in his sackcloth a little south of his belly button. She, curious, asked him what this bulge was. He replied that it was the Devil which must periodically be put in hell in order to drive him away. She innocently asked where this hell was, and he answered between her thighs. She readily agreed to put the evil Devil into hell. Boy, was Rustico a happy trooper but it didn't last long. She liked it so much that her daily demands to put the Devil into hell increased so much that poor Rustico ran out of gas and couldn't wait to get rid of her. Lady luck smiled on him and for some unexpected reason she had to return to the city.

Because the orgasm only lasts a short time, I guess the best way to world peace, as I suggested before, is giving all the people a long-acting happiness pill instead of an aphrodisiac. Which one would you guys choose?

The penis played a huge and open role in both Greece and the Roman Empire. There were statues and paintings displaying male genitals all over the place. The penis was almost always on everybody's mind and played a critical role not only in everyday life but on the nation's policies and strength. Look how Cleopatra seduced Julius Caesar and how it changed the course of history. I believe it was a famous philosopher-mathematician, Pascal, who said that if Cleopatra's nose were much larger than it was, let's say an inch or two, she would not have been so seductive and Caesar would not have sought orgasms with her and history would have gone in another direction. Also Mark Anthony would not have met his tragic end.

In Greece a man's penis was considered to be on a very high level having some kind of mystical power. Pederasty and pedophilia were very normal not only for sex reasons but also the belief that a man's sperm could transfer a mystical, masculine power to the young ones. (In a tribe, I believe in New Guinea, there's a modern similar custom where the early male teenagers must give oral sex to an adult male in order to swallow the sperm which would give them the mystical power to enter manhood).

When it came to adult males, homosexuality was frowned upon though a lot of it went on behind closed doors. If an adult male was sodomized he lost much of his male status and was treated like a woman.

Regarding the size of the penis, the Greeks preferred thin ones. (I haven't read anywhere a survey of ancient Greek women's opinions on this subject)! Aristotle wrote that the thinner the penis, the stronger the sperm. This theory has not yet been tested. In any event, regardless of size, the Greeks loved their erections. Plato called this a state of "Divine madness" but warned it can be "disobedient and self-willed." In my old neighborhood we had the saying, "The pecker has no conscience."

The Romans were all for large penises. Statues and other visual representations of the pagan god, Priapus, were everywhere. Occasionally soldiers would be promoted to a higher level, even generals, based on the size of their penises. Priapus was first conceived by the Greeks. He was the child of the Greek goddess of love, Aphrodite, and the wine and life-loving god, Dionysius. Well the Romans loved this guy because the size of his penis was about two feet long! The head of the penis is called the glans coming from the Latin word for bullet.

Romans with large penises were admired. One Roman wrote, "If from the baths you hear a round of applause, Maron's giant prick is bound to be the cause".

The Roman women evidently preferred the Roman style penis to the Greeks. The Roman writer, Marcus Valerius Martialis, composed the poem, Nulla Puella Negat or No Girl Says No.

> I've searched throughout the city,
> Safronius Rufus,
> To find a girl who says No.
> No girl
> says No.
> It's as though
> It were wrong,

Or disgraceful,
Or a sin,
To say No.
And so,
No girl
says No.

There is another way in which people who believe that the penis-sperm-orgasm connected trio is evil handle the situation. It's castration. In both pagan and later on Christian Rome, certain sects would happily have their penises, testes or both cut off. These dramatic acts are indirect expressions of the power and fear of the biological drive of man to seek orgasms. Such events have occurred in other cultures and, who knows, may be still happening today.

Now let's take an important look at Christianity's take on sex for it has been the major factor in determining the rules for having orgasms up until about fifty years ago. It's still a force in the U.S. but has lost significant ground but is by no means dead. The basic message is that male orgasms should be limited. It's a complicated story but I will try to very briefly boil it down to basic doctrine.

Christianity was highly influenced by the great Catholic theologian, St. Augustine, who lived in the fourth century A.D. In his youth he was a lover but had a sense that something was wrong with his lifestyle. He wrote, "Make me chaste, O God, but not now".

He then converted to Catholicism and developed the doctrine of Original Sin which is the first sin ever made by Adam and Eve and which everyone since then has been born with including you gentlemen. He believed that it was originally transmitted to Eve by Adam's semen. Since all folks born since then had their origins in Adam's semen it naturally follows that Original Sin was transmitted with it and is, therefore, intrinsically evil.

Now I know that this is tough for you to conceive of but this belief created a powerful negative image of the penis so much so that it disappeared from paintings and sculptors. Sexual activity of all kinds was severely restricted. It is interesting to note that Eve was not blamed. This is probably because no one knew of ovarian eggs for the technology was not there to find them. Who knows, if Augustine knew of these eggs, he would have included them along with semen particularly because Eve was the one who tempted Adam to commit the sin. It takes two to tango! On the other hand, something in me tells me that Augustine would have stuck with the semen.

Centuries later, another great Catholic theologian, St. Thomas Aquinas, though going along with Augustine's concept, appreciated the powerful need for a male to have orgasms and recommended that prostitution be legalized in order to keep men from going nuts and getting divorced.

All kinds of things happened but the ultimate result was that sex was to be restricted to marriage only. Masturbation, for example, was not only a sin but was supposed to drain your brain and make you a dummy – which has yet to be tested in human males! (Not much has been written on female masturbation and what it may do to their brains). Even after the Reformation when Protestant religions broke off from the Catholic Church, these restrictions were maintained by them. But the basic message was the less semen the better off we are. That means fewer orgasms.

You may be surprised to know the Mr. Kellogg, the cereal maker, and Mr. Graham, the Graham Cracker guy, teamed up together to produce food products that would discourage semen production.

Jumping ahead to the twentieth century, it was physician and inventor of psychoanalysis, Sigmund Freud, who revolutionized sexual thinking and placed the penis back on the national radar screen where it has remained since. Interestingly enough, his main thrust, pardon another pun, was how both penal activity and personal thoughts of the penis were related to neurosis and not pleasure. He evidently was not properly influenced by the ancient Greeks and Romans.

He coined such terms as "penis envy", where a woman wants one, to "Oedipus complex", where a son, in his inner subconscious and psychic depths, wants to make love to his mother and have an orgasm but is afraid of the father and has a subconscious desire to kill him. He believed that the real purpose of the vagina is not to have pleasure but to capture the penis. Shades of Rustico and Alibech!

His influence and popularity were enormous but have dramatically faded in the past few decades. But he laid the foundation for the attack on the penis by the feminist and women's liberation movements.

Most of you are probably not aware of the feminist movement which began over a half a century ago. It was the initial phase of what is now called the women's liberation movement which most of you know about and is still with us today. It became the major force that led to female competition against men which you guys are still living with and which I'll talk about later.

Regarding sex, the message was frequently viciously anti-male. Slogans such as "Who needs a husband for sex? And who needs a husband at all?" permeated our culture. Women's magazines frequently had stories about how women rejected men and were now with women in a lesbian relationship and happy as can be. Use of sexual penile toys such as dildos increased. In the final analysis we are dealing with women's attempt to control men's orgasm either directly or indirectly including an emotional attack against the penis. Speaking about the women's attack on the penis, many years ago the Welsh fought the English in vicious battles. I read somewhere that when an English soldier was mortally wounded or dead, the Welsh women would rush to the man, cut off his penis and stuff it in their own mouths. On the other hand, I read a different version of the story where the Welsh women would place the penises in the mouth of the dead soldiers and have the testes hang over their chins.

And what about today? You are now living in what I call DeFelice's Age of the Orgasm. You are happily sinking in it and better wake up before it's too late.

Young U.S. males, let alone the old-timers (Viva Viagra!), are having more orgasms than any other males in history. And though I am not "THERE" I understand why you guys are happy when the hormones are flowing. But, listen to me, what's involved in having them is like a double edged sword and you pay the price. One side delivers short term pleasure while the other oftentimes delivers more long term pain. If you don't believe me just look around you and observe how many young couples, including yourselves, are swimming in happiness or frequently having problems and suffering.

Up until very recently, most of our assumptions on how sex works, from the fertilization of an egg to prostitution in action, have been made by observation be it on individual acts or group customs. As I said before, photojournalism has enormously increased our knowledge within a few short decades. But now we are in the Age of Modern Science where we now have all kinds of exploding technology that can objectively measure things. Mathematics brought us 2+2 =4 but modern technology has brought us lots of new tools to observe not only the Universe but, shall I dare say, more importantly, sex.

The human mind has done a spectacular job in creating ways to stimulate sexual mating in order to have orgasms some of which produce more babies to propagate the race and others not.

The following is a partial list of acts, including the use of technology, that produce heightened male stimulation and bring about orgasms:

- Normal heterosexual acts between a man and a woman.
- Rape.
- Homosexual or gay acts among men.
- Violence.
- Fantasies such as domination and dressing like Little Bo Peep.
- Snuff movies watching a simulated or actual murder.
- Voyeurism.
- Seduction.
- Porn videos that couples watch together.
- Searching in cyberspace for the right partner or partners.
- Drug induced elimination of sexual barriers.
- Courses taught to increase the effectiveness of foreplay.

Science certainly supports what I'm talking about. Researchers at Northwestern University used fMRI or functioning magnetic resonance imaging which locates metabolically active parts of the brain to see what parts would react if exposed to what are called the seven deadly sins- pride, envy, greed, anger, gluttony, sloth (extreme laziness) and, the big one that we're talking about, lust. Lust means how you, as males, are powerfully driven to make love to a woman in order to have an orgasm.

Here's what they found: only specific parts of the brain became active when exposed to six of the sins. There was one exception and you may have guessed it right. It was lust! When exposed to this sin and unlike the other ones, practically the entire brain was lighted up and buzzing!! (Before I forget, in another study when discussing politics only the emotional part of the brain became active)!

I read in my notes that there was a study on men and women Internet users regarding how many of them watched porno to sexually stimulate them. The results were no surprise. About eight times more men clicked the porno channel.

You can be sure that men will think of more and more creative ways to stimulate their libidos in order to have orgasms which, unfortunately, will make them less competitive in life. Look, we now have Viagra which causes erections in both young and the old men and is not much of an aphrodisiac, if at all. There is little doubt that someday soon the first true aphrodisiac will be available whether it's for a man, a woman or both. In either case, when this happens the beginning of the Age of the Orgasm will be completed, and you guys will be in big trouble if you don't watch out.

Many of you are probably thinking, "Hey Doc, what treatment would you prescribe to protect us against the negative impact of too many orgasms"? Unfortunately, no acceptable treatment has yet been discovered. I would not recommend castration. The female hormone, estrogen, may work but you wouldn't appreciate the side effects such as enlarged breasts.

I would use as a guideline the importance of your self-interest and the Principle of Drawing the Line. For example, I enjoy drinking but I consciously draw the line when booze starts interfering in my life and, therefore, self-interest and you must draw the line early in the game in order to avoid developing a bad habit.

Tough to do? You bet! Could I draw the orgasm line if I were younger living in your world? I don't know, but what I do know is that I would surely try.

Where Do You Go From Here?

Up, up and away!

Superman

Now that I've concluded that you're losing in our competitive world you understandably are expecting advice from me on how to reverse the trend. Unfortunately, I don't have definitive answers but enough that might help establish the foundation of principles that I believe can help you a lot. I'll first give my opinion regarding your personal lives and then how do we handle the general anti-you movement and make you competitive again.

There are huge rapidly changing forces mostly driven by technology and the marketeers that are taking all of us to unknown territories, and where she stops nobody knows. For example, the genetic revolution has created the new branch of science, transhumanism, which is the way to make people "better" than they naturally are starting from when you're a sperm in the womb to being on a wheelchair in a nursing home. If you want your son to have black hair, be muscular and dumb you can make the necessary genetic alterations of the fetus. If you want an army of super strong and intelligent men, genetic engineering will do the job. In case you don't know it transhumanism has already begun. There are influential, yes, the moralists and the ethicists guys and gals, who are already developing the field of transhumanism ethics.

Not too far away in the future we'll be able to grow all sorts of people in tanks of nutritional fluid. If something goes wrong and the sponsor doesn't like what he sees, he'll order the technician to empty the tank and let the thing die. And, since most ethicists are pro-choice, they won't object because it is like performing an abortion. I don't believe the pro-life people will be able to save the thing by legal means.

There is also so much going on that we can only see some of the big things such as 9/11 and the Super Bowl. But little, unseen things can have enormous impact on our lives. For example, it is not unreasonable to assume that constipation caused by calcium supplementation taken by women is one of the major causes of divorce in the United States.

About a quarter of a century ago, expert physicians recommended that women should take calcium supplements in order to help slow down post-menopausal osteoporosis. Osteoporosis is the thinning of bone that commonly occurs in old age. You frequently hear of old timers falling down and fracturing the hip or shoulder bone which oftentimes alters their lifestyle in very sad ways until their final moments.

Though you rarely read about it, calcium causes constipation. To begin with, women are generally more constipated than men. Now I don't know about you, but when many folks are constipated, including myself, they become both irritable and irritated and in a foul mood which negatively impacts others who are around them and spreads like a virus to others. It is highly probable that millions of women who are naturally constipated become more constipated by taking calcium and experience negative mood changes which cause great friction in married life. It is no surprise that there is a correlation over time between increased calcium intake and the increase in the divorce rate.

Elderly men also experience osteoporosis but not nearly as much as women. For certain reasons, however, few men take calcium supplementation. It's probably because the marketeers focus on the much larger lucrative female market.

Although this book is not about medical therapy, it makes sense to take magnesium with calcium. Magnesium is both an important element of bone and can increase bowel movements. Tell your parents about this for it may save their marriage! So you see, little things can mean a lot.

Getting back to big things, technology such as nuclear, biological toxin and cyberspace wars and the men or women behind it also makes it more possible for sudden and major cataclysmic changes that will affect you and your competitors in one way or another. Bottom line, the future is just too big to see.

Do all of these doom and gloom scenarios make me a pessimist? Not really. It's just not in my nature and, you know, it's the scorpion thing again. What I'd like to talk about now is your present situation and some personal observations and advice.

You remember when I spoke about how difficult it is to prove that something is good or bad, ethical or unethical, moral or immoral by the use of reason? I did it in order to prevent you from being fooled by ethicists and other marketeers by their faulty, deceiving arguments. I would, imperfect as it is, prefer to rely on the thing called life's experiences to figure out what's good or bad. For example, if someone risks his life to save a drowning person, except for a few cynics, we consider this a good act. If a teacher spends lots of her free time to help a struggling student, or if a father and mother go all out to help their adult children in difficult times, we consider this doing good. If a man deserts his wife and children, we would consider this a bad act.

There is a general written standard, learned by experience, of doing good in many cultures which is based on the critical importance of altruism or helping others. The most famous in our country is the Golden Rule in which Jesus said, *"Do unto others as you would have them do unto you"*. This belief echoes in many other cultures with vastly different customs and beliefs many never having any knowledge of the other's existence which, in itself, supports the belief that there is a universal standard. Some other examples are:

"Do not kill or injure your neighbor, for it is not him that you injure, you injure yourself."
   - Shawnee Indians

"Whatever is disagreeable to yourself do not do unto others"
   - Zoroastrianism

"No one of you is a believer until he desires for his brother what he desires for himself."
   - Islam

"One should seek for others the happiness one desires for himself."
   - Buddha

There are many, many more but I've got to put in what my favorite philosopher who used simple observation of human behavior to build his model of trying to find the truth, Aristotle, wrote. *"You should behave toward friends as we would wish friends to behave toward us."*

And here's some new news that, would you believe, is, for different reasons, freaking out conservatives, liberal and lots of others. Some respectable scientists have proposed that during evolution there appeared all kinds of "mental" genes that make us behave a certain way and believe in certain things. There may now be a God-gene which is behind the universal belief in religion and an after-life of some sort. There also may be an altruism-gene which may be behind the reason why we stick together helping each other.

The cynics, those unhappy guys who, in my opinion, have big problems with women, can happily counter this possibility and say that there are war-genes, miserable-genes and all kinds of other bad-genes that are stronger than the good-genes. I have no problems going along with them but this does not nullify the existence of the God-gene.

Before I give you my opinion on this matter let me tell you a story of what happened in one great period of Greek history. The heavily disciplined and military Spartans from the south decided to invade and conquer the more civilized northern city of Athens. The leader of Athens, Pericles, who was the guy who helped bring this city to a high level of the great Greek civilization, went to the community square to explain his war strategy to the Athenian citizens. At that time Athens was a walled city next to water with a far superior naval fleet than the Spartans.

He explained to the Athenians that he decided not to directly confront the superior disciplined Spartan soldiers but to withdraw behind the city walls and fight short battles or skirmishes and then retreat behind the walls waiting it out playing it by ear. One of the doubting citizens asked, "Pericles, Pericles, is this right decision?" Though Pericles was a great politician- he knew all the tricks that politicians play- he didn't hesitate to tell the truth and nothing but the truth. He said something like, "How the hell do I know but we must do something!"

WE MUST ASSUME WE CAN KNOW WHAT IS GOOD OR BAD AND HOW WE SHOULD ACT EVEN THOUGH WE CAN'T PROVE IT OR WE'LL HAVE CHAOS. And now I'll make an effort to tell you what I think you should know and do. How's that for humility?

As I said before, I interviewed all kinds of folks and observed all kinds of scenes that are going on today to get a feel for what specifically is going on in your world trying to help you fight the anti-you movement in our country.

Just this morning I had four old-timers all over the ages of seventy-five over to my home to find out what advice they would give you. These gentlemen are a curious group. Every morning they get together at the local McDonald's for breakfast to discuss what's going on in the world and what can be done about it. You've got to remember that they were reared (this and not "raised" is the proper word) in the days of old time values that were very different than those we have today. It was not only a learning experience for me but I had lots of laughs and a wonderful time.

(One of the keenest observers of human nature, Montaigne, wrote that one of the best ways to both learn about and enjoy life at the same time is by enlightening conversation, face to face, around the dinner table with good food and spirits, and I wholeheartedly agree. This can't be done in cyberspace so I urge you to practice your dining skills).

Getting back to my senior friends, they lived in very tough times compared to today. Let me add that they are all strong men, self-sufficient and married to the same women forever. Like everyone else they got their share of being beat up in life. You guys ain't seen anything yet! But they are, I wouldn't use the word "happy", but rather satisfied with what they accomplished in life. Enviable men!

And would you believe that, though they're really worried about what's going on in our country, they are still optimists. These guys do not take pills for depression but, instead, aspirin for arthritis! (I didn't ask them about Viagra. It's none of my business). Your natural instincts may lead you to think that they are out of touch with modern life. Take my word, they are not. So pay attention and think about what they had to say. Though it may sound like simple, old-fashioned stuff there's a ton of wisdom in those words. Remember; if you don't listen you don't learn. I want you to pay particular attention and think, think and think about them.

Never pal around with folks who have no sense of humor. And if you can't laugh at yourself then you're doomed to dwell in a lower level of life.

The following is a summary of what I call the Nine Commandments of the Old Timers (ten would have been sacrilegious):

1. Be strong and your own man. Work hard. One of the gentlemen quoted Samuel Goldwyn, the famous movie legend, "The harder I work, the luckier I am."

2. Be considerate to others. Treat other people with respect.

3. Take care of your family first. Friends come a distinct second.

4. Be honest. Keep your word and don't be a squealer.

5. Treat women with respect. (These oldtimers still put women on a pedestal which pleased me)!

6. Try hard to find the right woman to live with for the rest of your life.

7. Stop thinking too much about yourselves.

8. Regarding our country be extremely patriotic and very pro-American. We should strive to be number one in the world, second to none, in every area from economic to military.

9. We have a duty to help others in the world but do it wisely.

Now I'm going to ramble all over the place. Let's start with patriotism and an example how DMS is related to our loss of patriotism. Our founding fathers were strong patriotic men who loved our country. Patriotism is primarily a man thing and was the fire in the belly of those statesmen who drove America to greatness.

About fifty years ago, about the time DMS was born, the attack on America by Americans and the decline of patriotism began. Now you see very few signs of its expression and when expressed there are those who now even sneer at it. The correlation of DMS and the decline of patriotism can take very subtle forms. For example, at certain sports events the Star Spangled Banner is sung – you know our national anthem. It is a very moving patriotic song that in the past was mostly sung by men with strong voices hitting those high notes with wide open-throated power. It was exciting! Now, many times, these men have been replaced by women with puny voices and sometimes even weak-voiced men who cannot deliver the vocal goods needed to bring about the uplifting, emotional patriotic moment.

Elvis Presley, the great one, was an avid and powerful supporter of patriotism. He loved our country. There is an interesting story about a meeting that he requested to have with President Nixon. Both of these guys were reared in big time poverty but managed to make it to the top in widely different - and I mean different - professions. Elvis wanted to help fight the war against illegal narcotics and wanted for himself a genuine badge from the U.S. Narcotics Bureau. (He did have problems with prescription drugs.) All the Washington security people were understandably against it but the two connected so well that Nixon gave the orders for him to have one. Before I forget, despite the consistent negative stories that have been written about President Nixon, he was patriotic, and that's one reason why the two connected so well and became friends.

I believe that one, huge cause for the loss of patriotism was brought about by a single book, *A People's History of the United States*. The liberal author, Howard Zinn, in addition to writing about the big events such as the revolution and the leading men, decided to write about the common folk emphasizing, however, how the leading men were kind of evil and screwed, or shall I say exploited the common people. He accuses the leaders of committing extreme brutality and even genocide- and he went overboard, big time. Its message is a powerful anti-patriotic one. In fact, after reading it, one young man told me that he almost felt ashamed to be an American. Luckily his father knew something about American history and set him straight.

About a quarter of century ago, this book became standard reading in high schools, colleges and universities indoctrinating- not educating- those young impressionable minds about the evils of our country. I understand that at least two million books have been sold, and God knows how many minds were and still are being infected.

I read that Zinn was a nice guy. But he didn't get it. No fooling, people sometimes do bad things and act out of self interest! It's human nature. The scorpion just won't go away. Always look at what comes out of the hopper or what I call "net effect" when thinking about a complex issue with lots of factors. Taking a broad view of history, in which country would you prefer to be born, live and die?

Winston Churchill, the great British leader during World War II, who understood human nature more than most men said something like, "Democracy is not such a good form of government but it's the best one we have." He clearly was aware of the scorpion!

Let's get back to DMS and take a look at one of the many relatively small unrecognized examples of it which all add up to a big hit. You are all aware that there's a big push in schools to have equal sports opportunities for men and women. But here's a dandy. I was having dinner with a friend and his seventeen year old son at a restaurant in upstate New York. The son told me that in his school women wrestlers have the right to join men's wrestling teams but men can't join theirs. (This is also true in certain other sports). What surprised me was that it didn't bother the young man. I told him what he didn't realize is that a new right has been given to women and his right denied. It's another disguised quota system. He told me that he knew of no one who has ever mentioned this point and would spread the word.

Now let's do some more rambling. I have a strong hunch that the prevalence of jealousy is much larger than recognized and has to be a nasty, disruptive and consuming force between men and women these days. Unlike in the past, many modern women have multiple sex partners beginning in high school until marriage. They understandably don't believe that sex is something special to be respected as they did years ago. It becomes a habit like many things we do- easier and easier the more you do it. So let's say your wife or your serious girlfriend is traveling and she's not a bad looker. Even those of you who may think you are a hot shot with women, take my word for it, there's always a better man than you out there regarding arousing the interest of a woman. And let's say she meets one after a hard days work at her hotel bar. Because of her attitude towards sex she would probably find it relatively easy to hit the sack with him without too much guilt, if any at all. There's also what I call geographic morality. It's more difficult to make love to your married neighbor in her next door bedroom than in a hotel room in Baghdad.

A couple of months ago a friend of mine told me something that almost made me fall out of my chair. He told me about a website of married women who were available to have sex with men, particularly in their neighborhoods, other than their husbands but they wanted to stay married. Contact information including sensual photos of some of the wives was featured on the website.

I found this hard to believe so I visited the website, and there they were! It is inconceivable that some of their husbands don't know about this. That's the subject of another story. Also, for your information, I didn't recognize any of the ladies.

Many men think about the aforementioned and knowing these realities would practically make most men jealous, and who the hell wants to be jealous? Jealousy is not an ingredient in the recipe of happiness.

Here's an interesting theory that dawned on me during one of my interviews with high school and college guys and gals. I always believed that the main reason behind the creation of the institution of marriage was to protect women by establishing a stable, sacred relationship with a single male. After all, men are sex crazy and physically stronger than women, and women would be vulnerable to physical sexual attacks by them. After my interview, however, I wondered whether I got it all wrong, and it's really the other way around where marriage protects men from women. You guys often heard about the bad *womanizers* in the liberal media. Let me tell you that what I call the *manizers* have come to town! So hold on to your hats and other things!

Let me change the subject for a second. Though I am not an expert on women, I have made many observations over the years. What common manly characteristics attract both traditional and feminist types of women? It's a strong male and don't let anyone tell you differently. And how do we define this creature? As I said before, it can't be done but women can easily sense it. It's the scorpion thing again. About thirty years ago when the feminist movement was in high gear and women were pushing their self-interest playing down the importance of men, there was a very talented feminist author, Erica Jong, whose book, *Fear of Flying*, was a huge success letting men know, among other interesting things, that women can also have their sexual fantasies. Now listen to this closely. She described how she meets a guy she likes who always talks about himself and his problems. She sympathizes with him but he does nothing to her hormone levels. Anyway, she turns to her fantasies and describes what she calls the *Zipless Fuck* which is when a man and a woman go at it like animals sometimes without even talking to each other. She remembers an Italian movie she saw where a sensual Sicilian widow and a very rugged, attractive Italian male soldier, whom she obviously considers masculine, who share the same train cabin but never met before and never speak to each other. Before the train enters the tunnel he slowly begins touching her in sensual but acceptable ways. When the train emerges from the tunnel it was obvious they had made whoopee. They both get off the train but she mysteriously disappears without ever having said, "thank you".

Erica Jong hit it right on the nose. Men who talk too much about themselves are perceived as weak by women. Today lots of modern men do talk too much about themselves either face to face or on Facebook and other means. You meet a gal and have lots to drink. You relax and you open up and talk about your life in detail. She, also talking too much, responds with her story. You are both on a high oftentimes believing that you met your soul mate. Now get this. For whatever reason, it's the scorpion thing, spilling out your emotions doesn't work and is a sign of weakness, and the lady will read and not respect this eventually lose interest in you and end the relationship. So stop talking about yourselves and learn to listen to your date particularly if the lady needs help in these unsettling times, and that's alot of ladies.

By the way, how can you guys talk about yourselves so much, for example, on Facebook? Don't you know that very few people in this world really care about you but they pretend to so that you will read about them? It's called in Latin a *quid pro quo* or "a this for that" or "you listen to me and I'll listen to you". Guys, it's another sign of male weakness which is now part of DMS and fueling the anti-you movement.

I bet lots of you think I'm off the wall regarding talking too much about yourselves. No so; and let me explain before you tune out.

Practically all, if not all, people desire or seek the need to be recognized. Recognition is a huge, natural factor that drives all kinds of behavior. You can see this in children showing off to women going to the hairdresser before a dinner party. Talking about or Facebooking yourself is a form of seeking recognition.

It's best seen in individuals in the entertainment, political and sports sectors among others. These men and women thrive on being recognized from a rock concert to winning an election. But oftentimes they receive so much recognition that it screws up their lives. I'll give you only one example but it's one that makes me think a lot about the negative side of seeking recognition. In the past, the movie actress, Judy Garland, who was a very famous movie actress and possessed one of the most beautiful voices that I've ever heard in the theatre, once lamented, "Why am I so lonely when I am so famous?"

So I'm not saying that the search for recognition is bad but too much of it is. And that's what's going on with you when you are into yourselves too much.

Look, you don't have to be a genius to realize that women, even though they are winning in the competition against you, are having rough times these days. Lots of them are suffering from TFS, or the Tension Fatigue Syndrome. You can observe it simply by listening to the ever increasing high pitched, rapid speaking tone of their conversations. They understandably like their new freedom but, as my psychiatrist friend pointed out, are paying a hefty price. Divorce has left many working women with the responsibility, in addition to being a mother, to have to work to cover the cost of living from the gas bill to babysitters. Also, having kids is a turn-off for potential male suitors. It's no surprise that more and more divorced women are swearing off getting married again and prefer to live the single life. It's just too risky for them, and I understand that.

Many women are dating or marrying younger men. They are called Cougars. This also occurs in the animal kingdom. Male chimpanzees in Uganda much prefer to mate with the old chimpanzee females.

Women in general are increasingly visiting therapists of all kinds for help. I am concerned about this for the simple reason that unlike doctors and lawyers there are no reliable standards by many of them to obtain a license to practice their profession. This in my mind presents a real danger for both men and women. In my limited experience, however, dealing with women with problems, professional licensed therapists have been solidly competent.

A lady friend of mine recently told me about a social gathering of high school football moms. They all shared stories about how difficult life is oftentimes but, thank God, with a sense of humor. What was surprising, however, is that they all openly talked not only about their problems but also about the pills they take ranging from tranquilizers, antidepressants and energizers to sleeping pills, and they were so happy to have these pills for they "couldn't live without them". Now listen to this, after discussing their problems some of them exchanged their medications thinking they were taking the wrong ones and needed the ones taken by their friends. There was one mom in the group that confessed that she took no pills and coped with life quite well. I found out later that none of the ladies believed her.

My lady friend suddenly burst out into laughter. She said that one of the ladies who underwent a long and brutal divorce experience suggested that in order to prevent such brutal divorces, every marriage license should have a mandatory expiration date on it.

Before I go on to offer some advice here's another story. I asked the oldtimers and about fifty or sixty middle-aged and elderly men what advice would they give to young, unmarried men like you regarding marriage. About one- third of them answered, "Don't get married" and another third, "Don't get married until the age of thirty". It is interesting to note that the thirty number was consistently mentioned by these veterans of life and for this reason you should respect it.

The Japanese men may offer some help to you during your delayed pre-marriage phase. They have their girlfriends or mistresses in bed or talk to them whenever they want. The ladies exist inside a video game and are virtually made to order. And made to order female robots are already on the way (male robots, I think, are more difficult to design!).

Now let's get to the bottom line about whether there is a way to not only stem the anti-you tide but to reverse it. One night, what I thought was a very creative idea, jumped to mind. As I mentioned before women are much better activists than men and maybe they would join the effort to support you.

After all, the U.S. military men – sailors, soldiers, fighter pilots, marines and others were either killed or, for example, lost their eyes or legs to protect the women and children of our country. Men did not want women to enter the battlefront but stay protected at home. So I thought that women would rise up to the occasion and join forces to fight for their men against the anti-you marketeers as the men fought for them.

I met quite a few of them. Though it was not at all a scientific survey, I'm kind of worried that the surprise that hit me may be generally true. Just let me give you one example that says it all.

A forty-five year old male friend of the family knew that I was interviewing women about their willingness to stick up for their men. He was hosting a dinner for four divorced women all about the age of forty. He invited me along to dine and interview the young ladies.

I arrived a little late after they had, let's say, a couple of swigs of wine. They were very pleasant to be with. I explained to them that the young men are taking a beating and asked whether they would be willing to join them in a counterattack against the marketeers who have planned and implemented the competitive successes of women, blacks and other special groups over you.

Wow! Was I surprised! They were all emotionally turned off by the idea. They were hostile and couldn't care less about you. I think I detected fire jetting out from both nostrils of one of them. Now you are probably thinking that their reaction was due to the fact that they went through divorces which generated hate and not love. But I did also speak to young married women and they responded similarly. There was only one group of women who supported you. They were traditional moms who had sons. How times have changed. There is little doubt that the ladies in my old Italian neighborhood would wholeheartedly support their men. But they were different times with different values.

The conclusion? It appears that you can't count on women to become activists for your cause. On the other hand, I'd keep an open mind for, if you haven't yet learned, women are oftentimes unpredictable.

Before I forget, I decided to leave before dinner was served. As I stood up and said "goodbye", one of the women said, "I understand what you are trying to do but we women have suffered too much goddamn damage by men." She then planted a heavy lingering kiss on my lips – I haven't the slightest idea what that was all about – but during that kiss I thought of Alexander the Great.

No one knows the real origin of the kiss. In some cultures it is even looked down upon. Not too long ago a Chinese newspaper cautioned the people against the invasion of the European kiss to China. They called it a "vulgar practice which is all too suggestive of cannibalism." One theory is that the kiss originated in India. When Alexander the Great conquered the city of Punjab in India, kissing was a very common practice, and he liked it so much that he brought it back to Greece. It spread like wildfire eventually infecting the Romans who went bananas over kissing - more than on the lips, may I add.

But there was a real problem with halitosis or bad breath and only after the dentist came up with formulas to diminish bad breath did kissing really spread.

Here's a tip. The soft slow and probing approach to the act of kissing will take you faster and farther than the alternatives.

I'm closing this book with a message that not only will drive the marketeers bonkers but spur them into launching a counterattack if the book becomes a success because it will threaten their self-interest.

A little more than a couple of hundred years ago, the brilliant Scottish philosopher, David Hume, said, "Certitude is for fools". In other words, you can't be absolutely sure of anything. Well, I want to tell you that I am a big "fool" for I am absolutely sure of what I have to say.

And here it is: DMS OF YOU, THE WHITE MALE, HAS LED TO THE WEAKENING OF THE COUNTRY so much that we now can't water board terrorists who have killed thousands of Americans and are trying to kill more or kill Canadian geese that can cause airplanes to crash. And it's getting worse. You see, male masculinity has been the foundation of the strength of our great country. Like calcium, constipation and divorce, this "fool" is certain that there is a correlation between what's happening to you and how our country is sinking into a state of self-destructive weakness. Guys, we are committing national suicide and the marketeers are the cause of it. In my opinion, unless something happens such as a national crisis, it's going to keep on going. And right now you are probably thinking, "If DeFelice is right, what the hell can we do about it?"

Frankly speaking, in my final version of this chapter I had only spelled out some general, vague principles on promotional or marketing strategies and left specific ones for your young minds both to come up with and implement. Fortunately, I had asked about a dozen fairly sharp ladies and men with diverse political and career backgrounds to review the manuscript for comments and criticisms before I sent the final copy to the publisher. Lucky I did for something rare and compelling happened. All agreed, from liberal left to conservative right, on certain issues. And when you come across this type of unanimity, you'd better listen.

The main points of agreement of the group were:
- That I outline a more specific marketing or educational strategy as a guideline for action.
- That the attack of white males is already generally recognized by a significant percentage of men and women which is a great advantage in marketing. Oftentimes you have to spend tons of money and effort just to establish your message at the beginning.

- That in this group there is a subgroup that can be characterized as a Silent Majority who supports the message of the book but is hesitant to speak out because of the current, aggressive anti-white male forces and the lack of support. But all, interestingly enough, believed that they can be mobilized by an effective message backed by effective leadership.
- That the weakening of America is already a substantial and increasing public concern shared by a broad segment of our citizens.
- That the connection between the attack against the American male and the weakening of America is not at all obvious to most. To make this connection clear is key to the success of the promotional educational effort.

Look, I'm not a humble guy but I do sometimes recognize my limitations. Regarding the first request regarding more specifics in the marketing effort there are men and women experts out there whose shoes I'm not worthy to shine. But reality left me no choice, and I had to give it my best shot.

One truly cold wintry night sitting by my fireplace sipping on my cognac what I thought was a brilliant idea jumped to mind. I said to myself, "Look DeFelice, the solution is obvious. Let's copy the marketing, educational efforts of the very successful Civil Rights and Women's Liberation campaigns."

The black leaders have been master marketeers, and I take my hat off to them. Boy, have they been successful in delivering the goods to the black community beginning way back around a half a century ago – and they are still at it. And what, in my opinion, was and remains the primary strategy is the marketing of "white guilt". In other words, whites are guilty of all of the abuses they inflicted on blacks from slavery to segregation even though some may be alive, most of them are dead, and current whites had nothing to do with black history. And, because of the truth behind the message, who could contest such abuses? Then the second part of the marketing message is that the country, based on feelings of guilt by whites, is obligated to make amends to the black people by granting them special privileges over whites in our educational system, getting jobs, and other privileges such as government subsidies. Bottom line we are talking about quota systems or reverse discrimination.

Knowing that they urgently needed national support, the second part of their original strategy was to create a mighty wave of public opinion giving white Americans insomnia over their guilt to create the change that they wanted. They effectively marketed their guilt strategy to the influential media knowing that many of these institutions are highly left liberal and would wholeheartedly buy this argument. Then the other institutions such as our educational system, particularly the universities, and government would follow. They hit it right on the nose, and the media led the charge not only to support the blacks but also, which you guys are not aware of, another campaign against the white male but, would you believe, not the white female!

The female liberation marketing strategy has been like the black one, a brilliant success continuing to score all kinds of points against you. Give our ladies credit where credit is due.

Unfortunately, after further reflection, it became clear that it was not such a smart idea the main reason being that ALMOST OUR ENTIRE SOCIETY, OUR LIBERAL EDUCATIONAL INSTITUTIONS AND THE STUDENTS WHOM THEY INDOCTRINATED INCLUDING MANY OF YOUR PARENTS, THE COURTS, THE MEDIA, THE GOVERNMENT AND LOTS OF OTHERS WERE ALREADY AND CONTINUE TO BE PASSIONATE SUPPORTERS OF BOTH MOVEMENTS AND THEY CURRENTLY WOULD BE AGAINST ANY MOVEMENT THAT SUPPORTS YOU. The costs and effort to even begin to dent this mentality would not only be enormous but frustratingly futile.

Well, after lots of thinking and discussions with some creative guys and gals, I came up with a promotional-educational effort which I call THE ME-YOU MARKETING PLAN. This ME-YOU approach obviously means a team approach where I must do my part and you must do yours in an all out effort. Now is not the time for mediocrity.

Let's start out with the ME-part, *Television and Radio Interviews*: For the record, let me first say that I didn't write this book to make money one main reason being that I don't need it. Whatever money earned will be used for the promotion of the book and/or its message. I wrote it out of real concern that our country is going down the tubes – just look at what's going on today - and that, in large part, it's substantially related to the attack on the white male and traditional masculinity values.

I decided to personally finance an initial promotional effort on the book primarily but not exclusively directed at television and radio talk shows in order to reach the Silent Majority of your supporters to educate them about what's going on and hopefully to stir the waters and find enthusiastic support. You may think that I'm contradicting myself because I just said that most of the main stream media will be against my message. Paradoxically, not so, for the message is, without doubt, highly controversial and controversy sells and selling makes money and, don't forget, media is a profit oriented business. They, as I said before, will probably try to label me as a misogynist or racist or whatever which flames the passions and interests of their audiences. There are lots of sharp men and women media folks out there who passionately oppose my message, and I'm prepared to take some big hits. I'm not as young and nearly as sharp as I used to be but as my father used to tell me, " Son, sometimes you've got to do what you've got to do no matter what the price you must pay."

I'm prepared to pay that price. The question is, "Are you?"

And now to the YOU-part of the effort, *Cyberspace*: Cyberspace offers us a wonderfully inexpensive way not available when the other two movements began to rapidly and effectively deliver our message by taking it viral. I have established my book website, www.DoctorDeFelice.com, which is the principal information and communication center of our effort including Facebook, Twitter and a blog. I hired a cyberspace expert to help identify interested parties. On the other hand, you must make a much greater effort to find individuals and groups that have interest and might support the effort bringing them to the website or independently. Because the subject matter is broad interest will be found in a number of seemingly unrelated groups ranging from mothers who are concerned about what's happening to their sons in our educational system to organizations that are concerned about the judicial violation of the principles of the Constitution. You should get together with your colleagues and think about potential audiences.

If our effort to spread the word is successful, then it is highly probable that leaders will appear and spearhead the effort to stem the tide of the anti-you movement and make you competitive again. Don't listen to the pessimists who claim that it's too late to alter the course of modern history. For example, they may tell you that the courts, including the Supreme Court, already have exhaustively addressed the issue of affirmative action and reverse discrimination against the white male and the law is more or less "settled" and judges would be extremely reluctant to revisit such issues. But the reality is that historically in our country, if there is a pervasive groundswell of public opinion on an issue, not only the courts but the government, our educational system and corporations among others will confront the issue. It's the Scorpion!

And it would help if you guys could wake up and light a fire under your ass and become angry over how you have been beaten up without anyone supporting you. Our two great presidents, George Washington and Abraham Lincoln, had vicious tempers which was a huge factor in making them move mountains. And don't forget, in addition to brilliant marketing strategies, anger fueled the successful Civil Rights and Women's Liberation Movements. Yes, as I said before, our culture now is doing its best to limit the expression of male anger but there is still lots of room left to maneuver.

Many of you out there undoubtedly have high enough levels of testosterone to energize yourselves to become leaders and get the ball rolling in order to stop taking a beating and become competitive once again. I challenge you to get out of your complacent world and perform a service for yourself, your colleagues and your country.

Well gentlemen, we've come to the end of the trail. You remember that wise old Socrates said, "Know thyself". I would add "Know where the hell you are".

I hope this book accomplishes much of both.

Good luck!

Stephen L. DeFelice, M.D.

P.S. I just got through watching the Super Bowl with my son, Stephen. In almost every advertisement there were dumber than dumb weak white males. When a famous advertising mogul, Donny Deutsch, was asked what he thought about the Super Bowl advertisements in general, he commented that he didn't like them because of the persistence in the ads portraying weak white males.

I forgot to mention my political credo or philosophy. It's fifty per cent conservative, twenty-five per cent libertarian and twenty-five per cent liberal. In what directions my tendencies swing depends on the circumstances and the times.

Today, my pendulum is swinging steadily toward the conservative – libertarian side.

LaVergne, TN USA
18 August 2010
193822LV00002B/1/P